170.42 Sin

Sinnott-Armstrong, W.
Morality without God?.

PRICE: $33.02 (an/m)

Morality ~~Without God?~~

PHILOSOPHY IN ACTION

Small Books about Big Ideas

WALTER SINNOTT-ARMSTRONG, SERIES EDITOR

This new series publishes short, accessible, lively, and original books by prominent contemporary philosophers. Using the powerful tools of philosophical reasoning, the authors take on our most pressing and difficult questions—from the complex personal choices faced by ordinary individuals in their everyday lives to the major social controversies that define our time. They ultimately show the essential role that philosophy can play in making us think, and think again, about our most fundamental assumptions.

MORALITY ~~WITHOUT GOD~~?

WALTER SINNOTT-ARMSTRONG

OXFORD
UNIVERSITY PRESS

2009

OXFORD
UNIVERSITY PRESS

Oxford University Press, Inc., publishes works that further
Oxford University's objective of excellence
in research, scholarship, and education.

Oxford   New York

Auckland   Cape Town   Dar es Salaam   Hong Kong   Karachi
Kuala Lumpur   Madrid   Melbourne   Mexico City   Nairobi
New Delhi   Shanghai   Taipei   Toronto

With offices in

Argentina   Austria   Brazil   Chile   Czech Republic   France   Greece
Guatemala   Hungary   Italy   Japan   Poland   Portugal   Singapore
South Korea   Switzerland   Thailand   Turkey   Ukraine   Vietnam

Published by Oxford University Press, Inc.
198 Madison Avenue, New York, NY 10016

www.oup.com

Oxford is a registered trademark of Oxford University Press

Library of Congress Cataloging-in-Publication Data
Sinnott-Armstrong, Walter, 1955–
Morality without God? / Walter Sinnott-Armstrong.
p. cm. — (Philosophy in action)
ISBN 978-0-19-533763-1
1. Religion and ethics.   2. Atheism.   I. Title.
BJ47.S49 2009
170'.42—dc22
2008055136

1 3 5 7 9 8 6 4 2
Printed in the United States of America
on acid-free paper

To Liz, Miranda, and Nick,
who show how good atheists can be.

CONTENTS

ACKNOWLEDGMENTS

Chapter Five here derives from my chapter, "Why Traditional Theism Cannot Provide an Adequate Foundation for Morality?" in *Is Goodness without God Good Enough*? edited by Robert Garcia and Nathan King. Various passages throughout several chapters here have origins in "Overcoming Christianity" in *Philosophers without Gods*, edited by Louise Antony. Thanks to these publishers and editors for permission to adapt these materials.

Chapters Four and Six owe a tremendous amount to Bernie Gert's insights in *Common Morality* and in *Morality: Revised Edition*. To avoid constant notes, I do not document every idea that I took from Gert, but my great debt will be clear to anyone who knows his work. I am also grateful to Larry Crocker for several of my best quotations as well as numerous helpful discussions and to William Lane Craig, Bruce Little, Dinesh D'Souza, and audiences at my debates with Craig, Little, and

D'Souza for showing me how evangelicals could best reply to my arguments. I also appreciate the financial and (yes!) moral support of Keith Augustine and Internet Infidels, who sponsored my participation in these debates.

Thanks also to David Lamb (who wrote his thesis with me on this topic and provided invaluable research assistance), to Jonathan Haidt (who made me rethink the value of religion), and to Peter Ohlin from Oxford University Press (who gave wise guidance and encouragement in this project among others). I am also grateful to Steven Schragis and John Galvin for enabling me to test my thoughts with a motivated and intelligent slice of the general public at One Day University.

For comments on drafts, I thank Eyal Aharoni, Larry Crocker, Bob Fogelin, Bernie Gert, Jonathan Haidt, Nate King, David Lamb, Andrew Mansfield, Peter Ohlin, and Lucas Swaine.

PREFACE: WHY THIS BOOK?

And now these three remain: faith, hope and love. But the greatest of these is love.

(1 Corinthians 13:13)

What's up with this title? Why is everything after the first word struck through? Because the goal of this book is to show that there really is no question about morality without God. There is just plain morality.

This point should not be controversial, but it is. Many theists are theists mainly because they believe, for whatever reason, that morality depends on religion. Some of them don't even distinguish morality from religion. The Bible separates faith from love (*1 Corinthians* 13:13), but many people who profess to follow the Bible see religious faith and morality as inseparable.

Unfortunately, the other side repeats this mistake. Many atheists and agnostics also identify morality with religion. When they give up religion, they also give up morality or, at least, objective morality. Richard Taylor, for example, writes, "the concept of moral obligation [is] unintelligible apart from the idea of God."[1] Such proclamations confirm the fears of the religious, but they depend on the same refusal to distinguish morality from religion.

This misidentification is pernicious. Our government needs a separation between church and state but *not* a separation between morality and state. We all know people who do not believe in any God or religion, and it will be very hard to get along with them if we assume that they do not believe in morality. If we do not get this distinction straight, our theories will be confused, and our lives will be contentious.

That's why I wrote this book: to try to help readers understand why morality has nothing essentially to do with religion. I was motivated partly by my experiences in classrooms. I give lots of talks to college students as well as high school students and the general public. Many of my students quote, "If God is dead, everything is permitted," attributed to Friedrich Nietzsche and to Fyodor Dostoevsky's character, Ivan Karamazov. The atheists who accept this dogma conclude that morality is subjective. The theists who accept this dogma conclude that atheists are dangerous. I want to show both sides in this debate that they are mistaken, and their blunder results from their shared but erroneous assumption that "If God is dead, everything is permitted." This book is an extended refutation of that popular slogan.

"You will never convince anyone, and you will anger both sides," my friends warn. That has not been my experience. On the assumption that "If God is dead, everything is permitted," people have only two options: They must either (a) believe in God and follow a religion or (b) admit that they and their friends are not morally good, and those who harm them are not morally bad, because nothing is really morally good or bad, right or wrong. Many people long for a third option, and it is easy to see why. Even if they believe in God, they still want a morality that they can share with their friends who do not believe in any God or in the same God that they believe in. Without some shared views about the content of morality, it is hard to see how friendships, communities, and countries can last long.

This issue cannot be ignored. Too many people worry about it. God and morality are among the most prominent and important issues in most of our lives. They are important not just today but also long ago, not just in your own local area but also around the world, not just to theists but also to atheists.

Unfortunately, both topics are also huge. Thick tomes have been devoted to only part of morality. Other thick tomes barely scratch the surface of only part of one religion. And, of course, there are many different religions around the world. I cannot cover them all. I want to keep this book short, clear, and lively. Also, I don't know enough to write about all of the diverse religions. Who does? Each religion requires years of study to fathom. So I need a focus.

I will focus on contemporary evangelical Christianity. Why? One reason is that I know more about it, having studied it and even believed in it at times. Another reason is that evangelical Christianity has a tremendous number of followers in the United States as well as a growing number in the third world. As a result, evangelical Christianity has become a powerful political force in the United States and other countries. It's not just that George W. Bush was tight with the religious right. So was Ronald Reagan. Recent democrats—Jimmy Carter, Bill Clinton, and Al Gore—were also evangelicals in many ways. Barack Obama was forced to broadcast his religious credentials, including a debate at an evangelical church, in order to have a chance at winning the presidency. Even after Obama won, he still had to appease opponents by inviting a well-known evangelical, Rick Warren, to deliver the invocation at his inauguration. Evangelical Christians, thus, continue to have a tremendous influence on politics in the United States, and they often push their political agendas by means of moral arguments. There's nothing wrong with this in itself, but it does mean that both evangelicals and their opponents need to figure out exactly how this particular religious perspective or style is related to morality.

What about other forms of Christianity? I will mention them from time to time, but I will not have them in mind except when I name them explicitly. Many mild and moderate forms of Christianity do not make such strong claims about morality as evangelical Christians do.

Traditional Catholicism, for example, claims that even atheists can know and follow the natural law, which does not depend on religious revelation. Additional moral prohibitions are based on revelation, so atheists cannot discover that part of morality, and perhaps they are not bound by those revealed restrictions. This Catholic view of morality is less prone to condemn atheists wholesale, and it makes the conflict between religion and atheism on morality less clear. That is why I choose not to focus on it. Still, I will bring Catholicism into the discussion at some points where it becomes relevant.

Milder religious views do not call for radical changes in our government, in our lives, or in our moral beliefs. Some liberal Protestants and reformed Jews openly admit that they are atheists, so their religion is more cultural than cognitive or theological. They clearly do not challenge my main thesis that morality is independent of religion and God.

Some new-age religions are downright unintelligible. It might make some people feel good to talk about "a higher order of existence" or a "guiding force or spirit." However, if that is *all* they say, such talk is empty. It does not really rule out anything, so no experience or moral insight could count either for or against it. It also does not matter much to most people. The kind of religious beliefs that pervade people's lives and lead them to take stands on political and moral issues must be clear enough to give definite guidance. There is no point in worshiping or praying to something as indeterminate as a "guiding force." No unspecified "higher order of existence" could save believers or help them get to Heaven or perform miracles or create the world.

Modern evangelical Christianity is much more detailed and clear. These features are advantages for its adherents, because they can tell how to follow it. They are also advantages for its opponents, such as me, because we can tell what needs to be refuted and what its implications for morality are.

What about other religions—Judaism, Islam, Buddhism, Hinduism, and so on? Some of what I say will apply to some of them as well. However, I will not try to sort out which of my points apply to which other religions. That would take a magic sorting hat, which exists only at Hogwarts. There are just too many religions to try to talk about all of them.

It is still worth noting that some religions do not postulate any personal God at all. They might even count as atheists on my definition. Polytheistic religions postulate more than one god, and some of their gods are immoral by their own standards. These gods cannot be the ultimate basis of morality, so these religions do not conflict with my thesis that morality is separate from God and from belief in God. That is why I will not spend time on such religions in this book.

Somewhat reluctantly, then, I will settle on evangelical Christianity as my target. Much of what I say will apply to other forms of Christianity and to some other religions, but adherents of those religious views will need to judge for themselves which of my arguments are relevant to them.

As the foil to evangelical Christianity, I will focus on atheism. Why? Because I am an atheist. I do not adopt atheism lightly or arbitrarily. I gave strong reasons for atheism in my parts of a previous debate book with an evangelical Christian.[2] That previous work rebuts the charge that atheism is intellectually irresponsible, but the arguments for and against the existence of God do not answer the current question of how morality relates to religion or God.

Even if some argument did show that God created the world, performs miracles, and appears to believers in their religious experiences, none of these arguments would show that God is all-good. After all, a very bad God could create the world, perform miracles, and appear to us. However, God must be good in order to be the foundation of morality. Commands from an immoral God would carry no moral weight, just as we have no moral obligation to obey evil human tyrants. Hence, none of the standard arguments for the existence of God suggests, much less demonstrates, that morality depends on God or religion.

On the other side, I gave three arguments *against* the existence of God. First, an all-powerful and all-good God is incompatible with the amount and kinds of evil found in our world. Second, an eternal and unchanging God could not have any effect on events within time, so He could not create the world or answer prayers. Third, if God existed, then we would have better evidence than we do for His existence. None of these arguments gives any indication of how morality can be binding without God, which is the issue here.

These arguments are also not conclusive. They don't pretend to be proofs. Hence, in addition to being an atheist, I am also an agnostic, in a way. You can, after all, be both an *atheist* insofar as you deny that God exists, possibly for strong reasons, and also an *agnostic* insofar as you claim that nobody (including yourself) knows for sure whether or not God exists. That combination is my view, so I am both an atheist and an agnostic in this sense. To avoid terminological confusion, I will call someone *secular* or a *secularist* when he or she is either atheist or agnostic.

I am also a relative *apatheist*, because I am usually apathetic about whether or not God exists. I do not spend my days worrying about God—either the traditional Christian God or Zeus, Thor, Krishna, or Allah—any more than I spend my days worrying about ghosts, elves, leprechauns, Nessie (the Loch Ness monster), or Bigfoot—or even advanced species on other planets. It is important to realize that most atheists and agnostics do not make their stance on religion central to their lives in the same way as many evangelical Christians do—and should, in their view. Except when I am writing books like this, the only time my thoughts turn to religion or God is when religious people raise such issues, such as by confronting me personally or basing public policies on religion.

Because I am an atheist, agnostic, and apatheist, I thought of starting a new club called the AAA, but that name was taken. For simplicity, then, I will usually talk about atheism and atheists. Much of what I say will, I hope, be congenial to agnostics and, hence, to all secularists.

Those, then, are the main protagonists in this book. It is written largely as a conversation between atheists like me and evangelical Christians. Our conversation is about the relation between morality and religion. Given the prominence of both atheism and evangelical Christianity in the modern world, I hope that this conversation will also be interesting to many others who are neither atheists nor evangelicals. Despite my specific target, much of what I say will have much broader significance, because the relation between morality and religion is surely a central issue for all religions.

Please do not expect too much. This conversation and my arguments in it will not even pretend to provide irrefutable certainty. I doubt that these issues could ever be settled to the satisfaction of all. They definitely cannot be settled finally by me or in a book short enough for me to write or for you to read. My main goal is not to convert everyone to atheism. It is only to show that atheists need not be arbitrary, unreasonable, ignorant, inconsistent, irresponsible, disreputable, uncaring, or, especially, immoral.

Morality ~~Without God~~?

birth and resurrection, in Heaven and Hell, or that bread and wine become body and blood (and then eat it!). Atheists often also see religion as dangerous insofar as it contributes to wars and leads to restrictions on abortion and embryonic stem cell research as well as to prejudice against homosexuals, women, and other innocent people. Who would want to marry someone who seems so uncritical, inflexible, and uncaring?

Of course, far from all religious people are uncritical, inflexible, or uncaring. Most atheists admit this, and all should. Atheists are often willing to overlook religious beliefs that are thin enough. Some atheists even join Unitarian Universalist congregations and accept their so-called religious principles:

- The inherent worth and dignity of every person
- Justice, equity and compassion in human relations
- Acceptance of one another and encouragement to spiritual growth in our congregations
- A free and responsible search for truth and meaning
- The right of conscience and the use of the democratic process within our congregations and in society at large
- The goal of world community with peace, liberty, and justice for all
- Respect for the interdependent web of all existence of which we are a part.

Atheists might have qualms about "spiritual growth" in the third principle, though the term "spiritual" is so vague that some atheists admit certain kinds of "spirituality." Anyway, the rest of this so-called religious declaration should strike most atheists today as fairly innocuous or maybe even positively inspiring. Thus, there's religion, and then there's Religion. Atheists can accept and even admire *some* religions.

Nonetheless, most atheists would be just as reluctant to marry any evangelical Christian as evangelical Christians would be to marry any atheist.

Of course, traditional theists *sometimes* marry atheists. I was an evangelical Christian myself when I met and fell in love with my wife, who had been an atheist since birth. Her tolerance of me at that time and for over thirty years of marriage has been amazing! More recently, a friend told me that his openly atheist son wanted to marry an evangelical Christian. Although she was well into adulthood, she insisted on getting permission from her parents, who were also evangelical Christians. They interrogated their prospective son-in-law vigorously for long periods on several occasions before the parents finally consented to the marriage. The couple is reportedly doing well so far, but the point is that tons of mutual doubt and fear had to be overcome, at least in their families. Some marriages between theists and atheists succeed, but the road is rocky.

How can these marriages work? Maybe the atheist really desires to believe or wishes that God exists. Maybe the theist really has doubts about religion. Maybe true love overcomes all differences. Maybe all of the above. Whatever the answer, such marriages are "exceptions that prove the rule" in the non-original sense that their rarity and difficulty prove that the rule holds in general. The chasm between atheists and theists is usually too broad to jump.

In many ways, these divisions are understandable and justifiable. Major religious differences suggest that a marriage is likely to run into serious problems eventually. Disputes about church, politics, friends, children, and even what to do on Sunday morning would probably arise often if an atheist married an evangelical Christian.

Marriage is just one example of this deep divide. It is a symbol of wider problems in our society. Would you ever choose an atheist as a business partner? As a lawyer? As a doctor? As a therapist? As president? This last question was asked in a USA Today / Gallup poll in February, 2007.[1]

If your party nominated a generally well-qualified person for president who happened to be ___, would you vote for that person?

More than half of the people in this poll (who were, presumably, representative of people in the United States) would not vote for an open atheist, even if well-qualified and nominated by the preferred party. "Marry an atheist? Hell, no. I wouldn't even vote for one."

TABLE I.I

	Yes, I would vote for that person.	No, I would not vote for that person.
Catholic	95%	4%
Black	94%	5%
Jewish	92%	7%
A woman	88%	11%
Hispanic	87%	12%
Mormon	72%	24%
Married for the third time	67%	30%
72 years of age	57%	42%
A homosexual	55%	43%
An atheist	45%	53%

According to another poll, only 14 percent of Americans believe that our country is ready for an atheist to be president. And Pete Stark is reportedly the only member in the history of Congress who has openly announced that he does not believe in any "supreme being."

This state of affairs is sad. The distrust between atheists and traditional theists forecloses manifold possibilities, not just marriages and political careers. More generally, the distrust between theists and atheists fuels misunderstanding and antagonism—even hatred. These deep divisions in modern societies get in the way of needed cooperation and progress. Theists rarely talk about religion with atheists, except when trying to convert them (for their own good, of course). Atheists avoid such conversations as well, because letting theists know that they are atheists might lead to personal repercussions. Atheists fear that their views will alienate or even scare friends and family members, as well as prospective clients and customers. Besides, atheists do not want to spend their lives talking about God any more than they want to spend their lives talking about other things that they do not believe in, such as Zeus, ghosts, and alien spaceships. Without discussing these difficult topics in ways that facilitate mutual understanding and respect, the situation will never improve.

Whose fault is it? There is plenty of fault to go around—on both sides. It does not help when theists tell atheists that they are going to Hell, that they are shallow (spiritually), or that they are immoral or untrustworthy. All of these disparaging remarks have been made about me to my face by theists who know nothing about me other than that I am an atheist. It is hard to keep talking to someone who misinterprets you as badly as this, even if the person wants to keep talking to you, which is rare.

Sometimes theists do not seem to realize what they are doing. When I published a very brief note on atheism in a magazine,[2] it elicited a large number of letters and emails. My favorite response (because it was so amusing) called me a "small minded" "egotist," "an arrogant fool," and a "pompous PhD," then added "it is pathetic that the College allows you in a classroom" and "That you don't [believe in God], I am sorry to have to inform you, calls into question your intelligence." Then it concluded, "Please be assured that this theist will impartially consider any persuasive response you can offer and, as such, I look forward to continuing this dialogue with you." Did the writer honestly think that I wanted to have a dialogue with a stranger who would say such insulting things about me in response to a short opinion piece? The critic had not even bothered to read my book, which was listed at the end of the short note.

My previous book on religion was a debate with William Lane Craig, a prominent evangelical, who also abuses atheists. In his opening statement, Craig wrote, "On the atheistic view, there is nothing really *wrong* with your raping someone."[3] I will show later why this claim is false. The point for now is that it is insulting. It also strongly suggests an unwillingness to try to see the world from the other point of view.

Craig is not alone, of course. To pick just one more prominent example, *What's So Great about Christianity?* by Dinesh D'Souza includes these pleasantries:

Atheism is the opiate of the morally corrupt....

When an atheist gives elaborate justifications for why God does not exist and why traditional morality is an illusion, he is very likely thinking of his sex organs. It may well be that if it weren't for that single commandment against adultery, Western man would still be Christian! ...

This is the perennial appeal of atheism: it gets rid of the stern fellow with the long beard and liberates us for the pleasures of sin and depravity.[4]

Funny lines, but, as my sister says, the key to the man in earnest is the man in jest. D'Souza asks atheists to debate him and many refuse. In his blog, he then calls them cowards and claims that they refuse because they have no adequate response to his arguments. Au contraire! They refuse because they do not relish being subjected to unjustified insults and slimy insinuations. Anyone who writes like D'Souza does not want to engage in genuine dialogue. Indeed, his writings undermine real communication.

These outrages might be dismissed as mere exaggerations by a few fanatics for rhetorical effect. But consider this response by George H. W. Bush (who might be the least evangelical president elected since Nixon):

Q: Surely you recognize the equal citizenship and patriotism of Americans who are Atheists?

Bush: No, I don't know that Atheists should be considered as citizens, nor should they be considered patriots. This is one nation under God.[5]

If atheists are not even citizens, much less patriots, then their views should carry no more weight in choosing policies for the United States than would the views of a citizen of Japan, Australia, or Zimbabwe. Why bother to discuss our country's laws with such "outsiders"? They can't vote here.

It is not only Protestants who dismiss atheism. The Catholic Education Resource Center prominently exhibits an article by James Gillis that begins baldly,

There are no atheists. At least no thinkers are atheists.[6]

Why talk seriously with anyone who is not a thinker (or who thinks that you are not a thinker)?

A different charge is made by the Christian Cyclopedia of the Missouri Synod Lutheran Church:

It is not possible for a man to be an atheist, in the commonly accepted sense, in his innermost conviction.[7]

This pronouncement denies that atheists are sincere. Why talk with people who do not say what they really believe? Compare someone who starts to argue with you about which candidate—McCain or Obama—should be president. You state your preference, but then he asserts, "You don't really want *him* to win, in your innermost conviction." How could the conversation proceed from there?

Of course, not all theists assume the worst about atheists. The examples that I chose are admittedly extreme. Still, there are many more theists who have no qualms about insulting atheists, and there are even more theists who stand on the sidelines and listen to such insults without objecting. They let more outspoken fellow-theists do their dirty work for them. These theists are partly responsible for the culture wars that they fight. They might not care. After all, Jesus reportedly said, "Do not suppose that I have come to bring peace to the earth. I did not come to bring peace, but a sword. For I have come to turn a man against his father, a daughter against her mother, a daughter-in-law against her mother-in-law" (*Matthew* 10:35). Still, whether or not they care, many theists do stand in the way of communication and resolution of this social problem.

Many atheists have contributed to the predicament as well. Christopher Hitchens named his book, *God Is Not Great: How Religion Poisons Everything.*[8] This provocative subtitle is an obvious exaggeration. It might make some atheists cheer and laugh, and it might help Hitchens sell books. However, it is not true, and it will not contribute to constructive conversation or mutual comprehension. Richard Dawkins called his book *The God Delusion,*[9] which suggests that theists are mentally ill, insofar as delusions are mental illnesses. Who wants to talk with someone who is mentally ill or who thinks that you are mentally ill? Sam Harris titled his book, *The End of Faith: Religion, Terror, and the Future of Reason,*[10] as if religious faith has ended and secular reason is the only future—or else that faith has terror as its purpose, in that Aristotelian meaning of "end." Even if we need to talk (or negotiate) with irrational terrorists, we do so reluctantly without trying to appreciate their point of view so much as to overcome them. And Dan Dennett's title, *Breaking the Spell,*[11] similarly suggests that religious people are under a spell (cast by a witch?). Earlier, Dennett among others labeled atheists "brights" and religious people "dims." Again, who holds serious discussions with dim people who are under spells or with people who announce that *you* are dim or under a spell?

Of course, you should not judge a book by its title any more than by its cover. I do agree with many (though far from all) of the claims and arguments made by Hitchens, Harris, Dawkins,

Dennett, and other "new atheists." The point here is just that their titles use a kind of rhetoric that can be fun for some, as well as an effective marketing tool, but is likely to undermine mutual appreciation. When atheists exaggerate and make fun of religion, they foster the image of atheists as shallow, crude, and even dishonest and immoral—certainly not friendly. They confirm and reinforce the negative stereotypes of atheists that many theists try to promote. These stereotypes are inaccurate, as I will argue, but they are widespread, and part of the fault lies with atheists themselves. Atheists who use such rhetoric can fairly, if only partly, be blamed for the culture wars that divide modern societies, especially in the United States.

Whoever is at fault, the problem cannot be solved without honest and open exchanges of ideas. All too often, atheists and theists move to towns or jobs or neighborhoods where they will not have to listen to people who disagree with them. Or they read books or watch news commentary only by people who agree with them. If atheists and theists continue to hide from each other, to refuse to talk about these crucial issues, to shut off their minds when others criticize their beliefs, and to block exchange by attacking anyone on the other side, then there is little or no hope for progress.

Both sides should agree that sincere dialogue would be useful. After all, theists think that atheists would find God if they just opened their hearts and minds. And many atheists think that theists would give up belief in God if they really thought through the problems with and for religious belief. Religious belief results from various forces, including emotions and social pressures in addition to reflection, but reason and communication still have some role in assessing religious beliefs, like other beliefs. If not, we are all up a creek without a paddle.

That is the spirit in which I offer this book. I am not trying to put down religion. I will often go out of my way to admit positive influences of religion and emphasize agreements between atheists and religious people. But I also want to have fun, and I hope readers will, too. What I say will, undoubtedly, offend many theists, since my position is that they are mistaken in what they regard as the most important belief in their lives. Nonetheless, we must be honest in order to understand each other, so I will not hide what I think of their beliefs. In criticizing their views, my goal is not to offend but only to approach the truth. I hope that theists who read this book will not be turned off or turn off their minds.

How can we begin communicating better? We need to start with trust. Imagine that the proverbial used car salesman tries to convince you that a car in his lot is a great bargain. You probably wouldn't and shouldn't even listen. Why not? Because you suspect that he will call it a great bargain even if it isn't, and even if he knows it isn't. You can't get useful or reliable information from people like that. Moreover, you would rightly fear that you might be harmed if you listen to him, because he might convince you with tricks, and then you might end up with a real clunker.

Similarly, if a friend tells you that a new model of car is really wonderful, you won't listen if you are aware that this friend doesn't know or care much about cars or that she has perverse values—preferring small, noisy cars that use lots of fuel. Shared values, mutual concern, and honesty are, thus, all essential for communication.

A show of respect is also crucial. If you start a conversation by insulting your interlocutor, the conversation won't last long and won't accomplish much. Just try it: Call someone a jerk and see whether he sticks around to listen to you.

These observations explain what experience confirms: Almost nothing turns people off more than telling them that they are immoral. That particular insult accuses them of being dishonest and of having perverse values, so it strikes at the essential basis of communication.

Yet that is what theists tell atheists when they say that morality depends on religious belief. Such moral condemnation widens the divide between theists and atheists. It also fuels the fears that keep theists from listening to and coming to know atheists as well as the fears that keep atheists from publicly admitting that they are atheists. Sadly, atheists whose professions depend on trust—doctors, lawyers, investment counselors, store clerks and owners, and almost everyone else—cannot openly announce their view of religion, because they are likely to lose customers and clients as long as theists think that atheists are less trustworthy than theists. That is a lot of customers to lose, especially in certain areas of the United States where evangelical Christianity flourishes, so many atheists do not announce or even admit their atheism.

There is also prejudice on the other side, for some atheists are reluctant to hire evangelicals or even devout Catholics in positions of trust. However, that is rare in my experience, partly because the majority is religious in the United States. Except in a few unusual areas, religious people do not have to worry that atheists won't hire them, buy from their stores, or become their clients.

In any case, my main concern here is with claims that atheism is somehow linked to immorality because morality depends on God or religion. By arguing against that common assumption, I hope to clear at least one obstacle out of the way of honest and open communication that hopefully leads to mutual understanding and appreciation.

My strategy will be to divide and conquer. The claim that morality depends on religion and God needs to be divided into five distinct claims. The first is that all atheists (and maybe also all agnostics) are morally bad. This comes down to an empirical description of the behavior or motives of individual people. The second claim is that secular societies— filled with atheists and agnostics—are bound to become corrupt and depraved. This prediction is also empirical, but it is about whole societies rather than individuals. The third claim is that objective morality makes no sense, has no firm foundation, or cannot exist without God. This assertion enters the philosophical realm of metaphysics or ontology, which studies existence. The fourth claim is that atheists (and, again, perhaps also agnostics) have no adequate reason to be moral. This claim is about rationality and reasons. The fifth claim is that atheists (and also agnostics) cannot know what is morally right or wrong without guidance from God or from religious scriptures or institutions. This final claim lies within another area of philosophy called epistemology, which studies justified belief and knowledge.

The following chapters respond to these five separate claims in Chapters Two, Three, Four and Five, Six, and Seven, respectively. Let's start with the empirical claim that all atheists are morally bad.

Chapter Two

WHAT'S WRONG WITH ATHEISTS?

The fool hath said in his heart, "There is no God." They are corrupt, they have done abominable works, there is none that doeth good.

(*Psalms* 14:1)

Atheists are sinners—no doubt about it. They deny the existence of God as well as the Holy Spirit. That denial is blasphemy, so it is enough to make all atheists sinners. Indeed, this sin is unforgivable forever:

every sin and blasphemy will be forgiven men, but the blasphemy against the Spirit will not be forgiven. Anyone who speaks a word against the Son of Man will be forgiven, but anyone who speaks against the Holy Spirit will not be forgiven, either in this age or in the age to come. (*Matthew* 3:28–29, *Luke* 12:10, *Hebrews* 10: 26–27, *2 Thessalonians* 1:8–9)

It is not clear why blasphemy against the Holy Spirit is worse than speaking out against the Son of Man. Is the Holy Spirit especially sensitive? And why are rape and murder forgivable, but not blasphemy against the Holy Spirit? Is blasphemy against the Holy Spirit that much worse than rape and murder? Is eternal damnation a fair punishment for blasphemy (even if committed by a confused adolescent)? But there it is, right in the Bible.

Such passages provide quick and easy routes to the conclusion that all atheists are immoral: Atheists are sinners. Sins are immoral. So, all atheists are immoral. Not just some atheists—each and every atheist is immoral, sinful, unforgivable, and condemned to eternal damnation, no matter how much good he or she did for others in need.

Of course, this biblical argument completely begs the question, because it depends on assumptions that atheists reject—namely, that denying God and the Holy Spirit is a sin and, hence, immoral. People who think that every word of the Bible is true must believe that all atheists are sinners, but this is no reason for anyone else to agree.

A theological argument is equally defective.

> If there is a God, he is all-good, all-wise, and truly great, and for that reason alone it is very good to worship him. But God is also our supreme benefactor.... Hence, it becomes a duty to thank God abundantly.... That means that grateful worship is a dominant obligation.[12]

From the viewpoint of theism, we all have a strong moral obligation to worship and obey God. He created us, so we owe Him big time. We morally ought to thank him for providing an ideal world to live in. We ought to admire his power, wisdom, and goodness. We ought to worship Him and pray to Him, as he told us to do. And, of course, we ought to obey Him. Atheists cannot do any of this because they do not even believe in Him. Doesn't this show that their lives cannot be fully admirable from a moral point of view?

No. If you know that another person sacrificed for your benefit, then gratitude seems obligatory or at least good. At least you ought to admit your benefactor's existence. People who refuse to recognize the existence of their parents, or who refuse to respect their parents when their parents are respectable, are less than ideal morally. But contrast a case where you do not know that your benefactor exists. Suppose you are caught in a bad snowstorm on the top of a mountain. You survive only because you find a cave to stay warm in. Suppose that a benefactor dug that cave in the mountainside just so that you could stay in it if you ever got caught in a storm up there. If you know about this benefactor, then surely you owe great gratitude. However, if you do not believe (and have no reason to believe) that any benefactor carved out the cave for your benefit, then there is nothing morally wrong with denying that the benefactor exists and refusing to express gratitude. That is parallel to the position of an atheist. Thus, if God does exist, then believers owe Him gratitude, but it is not immoral for atheists to refuse to worship, thank, or even recognize God.

In order to show that atheists are immoral, theists need to show that atheists perform acts that are immoral on non-religious grounds, so that even atheists should recognize their immorality. The Bible predicts that failure to acknowledge, glorify, and thank God will lead to such acts:

[S]ince they did not think it worthwhile to retain the knowledge of God, he gave them over to a depraved mind, to do what ought not to be done. They have become filled with every kind of wickedness, evil, greed and depravity. They are full of envy, murder, strife, deceit and malice. They are gossips, slanderers, God-haters, insolent, arrogant and boastful; they invent ways of doing evil; they disobey their parents; they are senseless, faithless, heartless, ruthless. Although they know God's righteous decree that those who do such things deserve death, they not only continue to do these very things but also approve of those who practice them. (*Romans* 1:28–32)

Atheists and theists should agree that murder, deceit, slander, and many other acts are immoral (for reasons that I will give in Chapter Four). Hence, if atheists are more likely to commit these kinds of acts, then they really are immoral in a way that should bother atheists themselves.

The claim that atheists perform acts of these kinds is a description or prediction of how atheists do or will act. It is also a claim about individuals, not atheists as a group and not secular societies. But is it true?

WHAT DO THEISTS REALLY THINK OF ATHEISTS?

Most theists whom I know deny that they really believe that *all* atheists commit acts that both sides agree to be immoral. After all, this claim would be both impolite and impossible to justify. So theists usually announce right at the start that they know some (or many?) good atheists. They even name their favorites. Dinesh D'Souza, for example, writes,

I have known quite a few atheists, and I am happy to testify that they can be good and admirable people. Both Hume and Darwin were famous for their decency and moral rectitude.[13]

Unfortunately, these admissions are usually tainted by qualifications and by conflicting assertions elsewhere. Just recall the quotations from D'Souza above and add this one: "Atheism is motivated not by reason but by a kind of cowardly moral escapism."[14] This claim is universal. D'Souza does not say that *some* atheists are cowardly moral escapists. That would be true, by the way. Some atheists are bad in that way. But D'Souza instead ascribes these goals and motivations to *all* atheists without limit. It doesn't seem to bother him that these claims contradict his admission elsewhere that some atheists are good and admirable people.

Other theists are less blatant. They explain away the goodness of atheists so as to give credit to Christianity. I have often heard veiled criticisms like this: "These good atheists grew up and live in a Christian culture. They have absorbed that culture. That enables them to be good, despite being atheists." Thanks a lot! That's like saying that some girls are good at math because they absorbed math from the boys in their classes. What a put-down! Why not simply admit that some atheists are good people? After all, other people get credit for their good deeds even though they grew up in the same culture. When theists explain away the virtue of good atheists in this way, it suggests that they really doubt that atheists can be virtuous on their own.

These doubts pervade common culture as well. Around Halloween, many evangelicals set up "Hell Houses" that explicitly display how horrible atheists are, in their view. They never add any qualification like, "Of course, this applies to only some atheists." Recall also the poll cited in the previous chapter. Over half of those surveyed reported that they would not vote for an atheist who was nominated by their favorite party and was well qualified. It is hard to think of any reason other than that many theists distrust atheists even when those atheists show how good they are. If the participants in this survey are representative, then a lot more people than admit it really do believe that atheists are immoral.

WHY DO THEISTS DISTRUST ATHEISTS?

Why do so many theists believe this? This prejudice might come from the Bible. The story of humans as fallen and lost without God's redemption and grace runs throughout the Bible. On a common interpretation, the point of the story of the fall from the Garden of Eden is that man and woman became rebellious and evil when they ate the apple from the tree. (*Genesis* 2:17 also says, "when you eat of it, you will surely die," but Adam reportedly lived 930 years.) Their descendants inherited responsibility for this original sin as well as a tendency to commit further sins. Remember Sodom and Gomorrah. The only way out of this curse of sin is Christ's saving grace through His sacrifice. Hence, only faith in Christ can help us out of our state of immorality (see *Romans* 3:28). That means that atheists are bound to be immoral, since they have not been redeemed by Christ.

The point here is not that atheists are sinners simply because they do not have faith in Christ. The claim is, instead, that their lack of faith in Christ leads them to do acts that even they should recognize as immoral—acts like murder, rape, lying, cheating, adultery, theft, and so on. Only love of God can lead them (or anyone) away from such a life, according to this view.

The same conclusion can be based on other theological premises. Many Christians declare that God is so obvious that anyone who denies God must have been taken over by Satan, so such people must all be dangerous. With Satan inside them, atheists can't be trusted. Christians often see the contemporary world as a struggle between God and Satan, just as some Muslims see the West as the great Satan.

Of course, atheists reject all of this. These theological dogmas might explain why theists fear atheists, but they cannot show that atheists are immoral in any way that counts here. Atheists do not accept the story of the fall from the Garden of Eden. Nor do they accept the view that the contemporary world is a struggle between God and Satan. Hence, it is cheating to use those assumptions as premises in an argument for the conclusion that atheists are immoral. It might be rational for theists to believe that conclusion, given their assumptions, if those assumptions are rational. However, those assumptions provide no reasons at all for anyone who is not already committed to the Bible or those particular theological dogmas.

Notice also that these theological arguments apply not only to atheists but also to agnostics and to people who follow religions other than Christianity. The question here is not only whether all atheists are immoral but also whether *all* secular people (including agnostics) and *all* followers of other religions are also immoral. The biblical and theological reasons for the claim that all atheists arc immoral would apply as well to all secular people and also to all non-Christians, though possibly not with the same strength. Thus, unless you really think that all non-Christians are immoral, you must agree that these biblical and theological arguments fail.

A FEW GOOD ATHEISTS

Whatever their reasons, and whether or not those reasons are any good, many evangelical Christians do seem to think that atheists are not morally good people. Of course, they are right—about many atheists. Many atheists cannot be trusted. Many atheists commit horrific crimes. Like many theists, many atheists are bad people. But that is not because they are atheists. It is because they are human. Any large group of humans has both good members and bad members. That holds for Christians as well as for followers of other religions, and it also holds for atheists and agnostics.

While many atheists are bad people, many other atheists are good people. Here are a few famous people who are reported to be atheists and seem pretty good: Isaac Asimov, Francis Crick, Marie Curie, Thomas Edison, Abraham Maslow, George Orwell, Linus Pauling, James Randi, Carl Sagan, Amartya Sen, Elizabeth Cady Stanton, Penn (Jillette) and Teller, Alan Turing, Mark Twain, Kurt Vonnegut, and James Watson. For more, see http://en.wikipedia.org/wiki/Lists_of_atheists.[15]

Of course, any name on this list could be questioned. None of these famous atheists is perfect. Who is? (Remember *John* 8:7: "If any one of you is without sin, let him be the first to throw a stone at her.") Still, many of these individuals led exemplary lives of service and contributed greatly to the social

which is or should be a value for theists as well as atheists and agnostics. Homosexuals usually do not bother their neighbors, much less practice pedophilia, as some unfounded and vicious rumors suggest. Of course, religious believers might cite biblical prohibitions on homosexuality (*Leviticus* 18:22, 20:13; *Romans* 1:26–27), but it is cheating to cite peculiarly religious restrictions here to show that secular societies are corrupt. Nobody would accept those assumptions if they did not already believe in the conclusion, so such arguments get nowhere.

There will be more to say about homosexuality (in Chapters Four and Five), but the point for now should be clear: Atheists and agnostics need not be bothered if secularization increases behaviors that they do not see as immoral. This point applies not only to dancing and eating pork but also to abortion, contraception, and divorce, which only some atheists and agnostics see as signs of social malaise. In the absence of any shared nonreligious basis for calling such acts immoral, they cannot be neutral tests of depravity. Even if acts like these are more common in secular societies, that alone would not be enough to show that secular societies are decadent. Religious believers might see such societies as degenerate. Some nonbelievers might agree. Their view might be defensible or even justified. Still, this cannot be the basis for an argument that would or should convince other people who do not share their moral assumptions.

Nonetheless, atheists and agnostics should be bothered if secularization did lead to behaviors that atheists and agnostics themselves recognize as immoral. But does it? We need to survey a variety of acts.

HOMICIDE

Atheists, agnostics, and theists should all agree that murder is morally wrong (for reasons to be given in Chapter Four). Homicide rates, then, provide one neutral test of whether secular societies are corrupt in a way that should bother atheists and agnostics.

Recent findings on this issue might be surprising. Gregory Paul analyzed a survey of 23,000 people in seventeen developed democracies.[21] The countries with high rates of religiosity tended to have higher (not lower!) rates of homicide, juvenile mortality (including suicide), sexually transmitted disease, and adolescent pregnancy and abortion. The United States and Portugal are religious societies that stand out in these respects in contrast with Sweden and Japan, which are more secular. The same contrasts hold within the United States between more secular areas, such as New England, and more religious areas, such as the South, where these rates were higher.

Of course, Paul's study does not prove that religion causes immorality. Other differences among the countries could explain the high homicide rates in religious countries. The most careful response to Paul, by Gary Jensen,[22] looks at even more countries (over 40) and uses sophisticated multiple regression analysis to separate the effects of many different factors, such as poverty and education. Jensen finds that intensity of religious belief is positively correlated with higher homicide rates. He also finds that the combined belief in both God and the Devil is positively correlated with higher homicide rates. However, non-intense belief in God alone (without the Devil) is not related to higher homicide rates than in secular societies. Thus, it is not clear that belief in God per se leads to higher homicide rates.

Why are such religious beliefs correlated with homicide? The statistics do not say. Some speculations are that (a) religion leads to moral dogmatism, which people use to justify private revenge; or that (b) religious people think they will be forgiven as long as they have faith in God; or that (c) they can blame their own bad acts on the Devil's influence, so it is not really their own personal fault; or that people who live in harm-filled societies (d) need religion to give them hope or (e) think that humans are bad by nature and so need to be redeemed by God. Perhaps most plausibly, (f) people tend to believe that the Devil exists when they see lots of murder going on around them. All of these explanations are speculations, however. To choose among them, we would need more empirical evidence and analysis.

In any case, these recent studies present substantial evidence that belief in God at least does not *lower* homicide rates (or the other kinds of "immorality" in Paul's study). Thus, they undermine the common claim that our communities will sink into chaos and corruption if too many citizens give up their religious beliefs and become atheists or agnostics. Moral depravity does not pervade secular Sweden or Japan, so why fear that anywhere else will degenerate if it becomes secular?

A different kind of homicide occurs in unjust wars. Atheists often claim that religion fuels aggressive wars, both because it exacerbates antagonisms between opponents and also because it gives aggressors confidence by making them feel as if they have God on their side. Lots of wars certainly look as if they are motivated by religion. Just think about conflicts in Northern

Ireland, the Middle East, the Balkans, the Asian subcontinent, Indonesia, and various parts of Africa. However, none of these wars is exclusively religious. They always involve political, economic, and ethnic disputes as well. That makes it hard to specify how much role, if any, religion itself had in causing any particular war. Defenders of religion argue that religious language is misused to justify what warmongers wanted to do independently of religion. This hypothesis might seem implausible to some, but it is hard to refute, partly because we do not have enough data points, and there is so much variation among wars. In any case, the high number of apparently religious wars at least suggests that secular societies are unlikely to be *more* prone to murder in war.

LESSER CRIMES

What about other crimes? Here studies are mixed. One meta-analysis of sixty studies concluded that people who believe in and regularly practice a religion are somewhat less likely to engage in crime.[23] The relation, however, seems to vary with kind of crime. One study suggests that religion is related to fewer "victimless" crimes (such as drug use and consensual premarital sex) but not to fewer crimes with victims.[24] Another study surveyed seventy-five metropolitan areas in the United States and found religion to be associated with less larceny, burglary, and assault but no less murder or rape.[25] Location also seems to matter. Studies conducted where organized religion is strong tend to find a relation between increased religion and reduced crime, whereas studies conducted in areas where organized religion is weak tend to find no relation (or only a very weak relation) between religion and crime, according to one review.[26]

All of these studies reveal only correlations. They do not show that religious belief or practice reduces crime. The causal train might run in the other direction. Maybe juvenile delinquents are less likely to obey their parents when their parents tell them to go to church, so they end up going to church less.

It is also plausible that adults who commit crimes or make friends with criminals are less inclined to attend church, because they find it tiresome to go to church every week and keep getting told that they are sinners. So they go to church less often or even become agnostics or atheists. A tendency for criminals to leave religion could explain why religious people commit less crime, even if religion does not cause anyone to commit less crime. Current studies do not rule out such alternative causal hypotheses, so they do not really support the claim that religion reduces crime at all. Crime might reduce religion instead of religion reducing crime. We just don't know.

We also do not know whether religious belief matters apart from religious community. In almost all of the studies, the correlations were between reduced crime and church attendance. Why would that be? Maybe because people who go to church are social—they like other people—so they want to avoid harming other people. Religious believers who avoid church are more likely to be anti-social loners. Or maybe people who attend church every week get reminded there of the importance of morality and caring for others. Sermons often include good moral messages, and such reminders can shape behavior.[27] If anything like this explains the correlations, then belief in God has nothing to do with it. Atheists and agnostics can join communities that regularly remind each other of the importance of morality, and this will reduce their rate of immorality without their believing in God.

As I said, we do not know whether this would work, because we do not understand the causal mechanism. Indeed, we do not even understand the correlations, and they are modest at best. So my main point is only that these studies do not provide any real support for the claim that secular societies are doomed to depravity.

ABUSE

To the contrary, some crimes seem to be increased by religion. If so, secular societies will include fewer of these particular crimes.

One example is sexual abuse by clergy, especially but not exclusively Catholic priests. The victims can be nuns or other clergy, but often include young boys and girls. One study estimates that 2 percent of priests are pedophiles,[28] which would be around nine hundred priests in the United States, but this number is speculative. More than three hundred lawsuits have been filed.

Some atheists take great pleasure in bringing up sexual abuse by clergy, because it exemplifies the depths to which religious people can sink. However, as I have emphasized before, we are all humans, so it should not be surprising that many religious people go very bad. The question is whether religion exacerbates the problem.

Some aspects of the Catholic church, such as vows of celibacy and strict hierarchies, might contribute to the rate of abuse by clergy. Perhaps more pedophiles become priests as a way of fighting their desires for sex with children but then find themselves in intimate circumstances with children who trust them and who will not be able to report sexual encounters, partly because of doubts of being believed, given the high esteem for priests. This hypothesis suggests that it is particular institutions, rather than belief in God, that create this problem. If so, the institutions might need reform, but these sad events do not show anything about religions without such institutions.

On the other hand, the problem of sexual abuse is not limited to Catholic priests. About 75 percent of Methodist clergywomen and also of female rabbis indicate sexual abuse by male clergy, according to one study.[29] So this problem might be due to something about religion in general rather than the institutions of any particular religion. We do not know.

Domestic abuse is a separate issue. The Bible is basic for all Christians, and it seems to endorse what would be considered child abuse today:

Do not withhold discipline from a child; if you punish him with the rod, he will not die. Punish him with the rod and save his soul from death. (*Proverbs* 23:13–14: see also 13:24, 20:30)

The Bible also endorses a fixed hierarchy among spouses:

Now as the church submits to Christ, so also wives should submit to their husbands in everything. (*Ephesians* 5:24; see also *Colossians* 3:18, *1 Peter* 3:1)

"Everything"! Must wives submit to beatings? Marital rape? Verbal and psychological abuse? Financial domination? The

Bible does not say so explicitly, and many churches have taken strong stands against domestic abuse, but it is still easy to imagine how abusive fathers and husbands would interpret the Bible as justifying abuse.

Do they? That depends. Several surveys have found correlations between more frequent church attendance and less domestic abuse.[30] As before, these are only correlations, so they could reflect a tendency for abusers to stop going to church or stop their spouses from going to church, where the abuse might be revealed. This relation also seems to vary among Christian denominations. In one study, conservative Protestant women reported more abuse than other women.[31] Another study found that fundamentalist Protestants were more likely to report being sexually abused by a relative, though non-religious and liberal religious participants were likely to report being abused by a non-relative.[32] Such confusing findings raise questions and exclude confidence in any simple conclusion.

Another basis for skepticism concerns the definition of abuse. Many cases of abuse are immoral according to both sides, but some other cases might be unclear. Different studies count different behaviors, and many rely on self-report, which leaves the definition of abuse unclear. Is spanking child abuse? The law says that it is if it leaves bruise, but that hardly matters morally. Is it abuse when a husband controls his wife by withholding their money or by loudly denouncing her for disobeying him? Such domination strikes me as unfair, but it might not be seen as abuse or as immoral by some who take the Bible literally when it says, "Wives should submit to their husbands in everything" (*Ephesians* 5:24). But then it might seem illegitimate to count such behaviors against religion, just as it was illegitimate to count homosexuality against secular society. To determine whether and how secularization and religion are related to morality, it is better to stick to examples that both sides see as immoral.

CHEATING

Let's move beyond violent crime. Another good test case for whether secularization leads to immorality is cheating and lying, since atheists and agnostics agree with theists that cheating and lying are immoral. Several studies have found that highly religious people report that they cheated less than atheists and agnostics reported that they cheat. Other studies, however, found the opposite for lying, namely, that more religious people reported lying more often than less religious people.[33]

Unfortunately, these studies depend on self-reports. The fact that one group *reports* that they cheated less often does not mean that they *really did* cheat less often. It would not be surprising if cheaters forget or lie about how often they cheat. Indeed, one study[34] of more than 14,000 adolescents found that 13 percent reported having taken a public or written pledge to remain a virgin until marriage. More than half of that 13 percent denied a year later that they had ever taken such a pledge. This denial rate was 73 percent among those who had sex in the intervening year and 42 percent among those who called themselves "born-again Christians" in the first year. Also, among those who admitted in the first year that they were *not* virgins, 28 percent of those who had taken virginity pledges in the intervening year and 18 percent of

those who had become "born-again Christians" in the intervening year later claimed in the second year that they *were*
(had become?) virgins. This shows how unreliable self-reports
can be in surveys about pledges and cheating. Thus, in order
to determine whether religion reduces actual cheating or
lying, experimenters need to devise ingenious ways to determine rates of actual cheating.

Some classic studies measured the rates of peeking during eyes-closed tests and of changing answers when students
were allowed to grade their own tests.[35] They found no relationship between religion and cheating in a large sample of
11,000 students.

In a more recent study,[36] a teaching assistant intentionally gave students one more point than they deserved on a
quiz. Students were then told that they might have received
an extra point by mistake, so they should regrade their own
quizzes and write on the top of the next assignment either
"I owe you a point," "Quiz graded correctly," or "You owe
me a point." Out of 130 students, only 32 percent honestly
admitted receiving the extra point, 52 percent said that the
grade was correct, and 16 percent actually tried to get another
point. The researchers had obtained background information
on religious beliefs, and they found that the one-point error
was honestly reported by 45 percent of those who attended
church weekly or more often but by only 13 percent of those
who attended church once a year or less. This study, thus, suggests that people who are more religious do cheat less often
than less religious people.

It would be a mistake to put too much emphasis on one
small study. Replication in larger and more diverse samples
is needed. It is also worth mentioning that even if religious

people cheat less, they still cheat a lot. It's not as if religion makes people honest.

Still, if this result holds up, then atheists will have to admit that people who go to church more often do cheat less. Does this show that religious belief makes people cheat less? No. As before with crime, the causal train might run in the other direction. People who are inclined to cheat and perform other kinds of immoral acts might attend church less often or even become agnostics or atheists. If that's the real story, then religion does not make people cheat less. It makes cheaters less religious. Again, we don't know.

DISCRIMINATION

Some religions teach that we are all God's children, so we should all be treated equally or at least fairly. Atheists and agnostics might seem to lack such a solid basis for condemning discrimination, prejudice, and intolerance. D'Souza goes even further when he claims, "The death of Christianity must also mean the gradual extinction of values, such as human dignity, the right against torture, and the rights of equal treatment asserted by women, minorities, and the poor."[37]

D'Souza gives no empirical evidence for this prediction. His fear, thus, might exemplify the common mistake of basing predictions about your opponents on your own internal sense of how those other people think and feel. We all—atheists and theists alike—need to learn to listen and observe instead of trying to feel our way into the lives of people who seem distant to us.

The scientific literature tells the opposite story. One review concludes:

> Using a variety of measures of piety—religious affiliation, church attendance, doctrinal orthodoxy, rated importance of religion, and so on—researchers have consistently found positive correlations with ethnocentrism, authoritarianism, dogmatism, social distance, rigidity, intolerance of ambiguity, and specific forms of prejudice, especially against Jews and blacks.[38]

To Jews and blacks, we can add women and homosexuals. Much of this prejudice is based on the Bible, which condemns homosexuality (*Romans* 1:26–27), blames Jews for the crucifixion of Jesus (*Matthew* 27:20–23; *Mark* 15:11–14; *Luke* 23:20–23; *John* 19:4–16), and prohibits women speaking in church (*1 Corinthians* 14:33–35; *1 Timothy* 2:12)—all in the New Testament. Discrimination is also officially built into many religious institutions, such as when women are not allowed to become priests.

Other passages send opposite messages, and many Christians, including many evangelicals, do not share these prejudices and even fight against them. I gladly admit all of that. There are many good evangelicals. But then we still need to ask whether religion has a general association with prejudice, discrimination, and intolerance that good religious individuals overcome.

Many studies suggest an association between religion and discrimination, but the degree varies. Some groups of church-goers have been found to be less prejudiced than others, but none has been found to be less prejudiced than nonreligious people.[39] One recent study, however, does find that "devotional religiosity independently predicts tolerance and rejection of scapegoating" although still "coalitional religiosity independently predicts intolerance and scapegoating."[40] When religion is related to prejudice and discrimination, the strongest relationships are with religious fundamentalism.[41] These are only correlations, however, so we cannot infer that fundamentalism causes prejudice. It is just as possible that people with prior prejudices tend to leave other religious orientations and turn to fundamentalism.

This talk of "prejudice" and "discrimination" is, admittedly, not always neutral. Religions that condemn homosexuality as immoral will deny that their so-called prejudice or discrimination against homosexuals is illegitimate. In their view, they are fighting immorality. The same goes, presumably, when they "discriminate" against atheists. They might also claim that it is not unjustified prejudice or discrimination to prevent women from becoming priests, require them to obey their husbands, and forbid them to speak in church, because their scriptures command this. They are not themselves prejudiced simply because they do what God told them to do, in their view.

It is not clear how far this defense goes. When two gay-bashers tortured Matthew Shepard and left him to die on a fence, some religious zealots defended this murder by citing *Leviticus* 20:13: "If a man lies with a man, ... they must be put to death." Slavery has also been defended by citing the Bible. And, of course, anti-Semites often cite biblical passages to justify discrimination against Jews to the point of genocide. Nonetheless, if religion is related to such extreme prejudice, then that should and would trouble most religious believers (just as Stalin and Mao should and do trouble atheists).

Even when discrimination, prejudice, and intolerance are less dramatic, the secular perspective remains very different. The forms of discrimination and intolerance that are justified by religious scriptures and rules might not seem unfair to religious people who accept that religion, but those acts still do seem unfair to people outside of those religions. If secular societies have less discrimination and intolerance of these kinds, then secular societies will seem better, not worse, than religious societies, at least to secular people.

CHARITY

Simply not killing, stealing, abusing, cheating, and discriminating is not enough to make you morally good. Morally good people also perform positive acts of helping the needy, according to most atheists and agnostics as well as theists. Thus, if secular people and societies do not help the needy, they lack moral goodness. A lower rate of helping the needy by secular people would hardly reveal the kind of depravity and degradation that so many theists fear from secular culture, but it would still be a serious defect.

Secular people and societies are morally deficient in just this way, according to a recent popular book by Arthur Brooks: "Religious people were 25 percentage points more likely to give than secularists (91 to 66 percent). Religious people were also 23 points more likely to volunteer (67 to 44 percent)."[42] The discrepancy looks larger for amounts donated: "In 2000, religious people—who, per family, earned exactly the same amount as secular people, $49,000—gave about 3.5 times more money per year (an average of $2210 versus $642). They also volunteered more than twice as often (12 times per year versus 5.8 times)."[43] Of course, many donations by religious people are to religious causes, but the difference remains when we leave out religious donations, claims Brooks: "Religious people are more charitable in every measurable nonreligious way—including secular donations, informal giving, and even acts of kindness and honesty—than secularists."[44] It is worth spending time on Brooks's argument, because it has attracted a lot of attention and is repeated by many evangelicals.

To assess Brooks's generalizations, we need to dig deeper. In particular, we need to ask *why* religious people donate more to charities. Brooks avoids this question, because "judging motives is misguided. Charity is a behavior, not a motive."[45] He is clearly correct that behaviors are different from motives. It is disingenuous, however, to criticize "judging motives" in a book titled *Who Really Cares*. Caring is about motives, not behavior. Thus, if we want to find out who really cares, we must ask about motives.

Motives are difficult to pinpoint, but there is little doubt that expected rewards and punishments affect not only behaviors but also motives in many people. The Bible says that those who help the needy will receive "eternal life" whereas those who fail to help the needy will suffer "eternal punishment" (*Matthew* 25:46; see also *Luke* 6:38). Since these verses are well known, it seems likely that many religious people donate more to charity than they otherwise would at least partly in order to buy their way into Heaven or buy their way out of Hell. Of course, this motive is not shared by all religious people—probably not even most. Many religious people work hard and long for charities in order to help the needy, not just to help themselves. Still, while some religious people are good, others are not so good, and the bad ones probably have bad motives.

Several religious traditions also specifically require tithing (*Leviticus* 27:30). When tithing is demanded as a strict duty, whose fulfillment is rewarded by Heaven and whose violation is punished by Hell, then it should not be surprising that many believers tithe and that their motive is often (though not always) their own self-interest.

Forced gifts, however, bring no moral credit. Imagine that an employee gives a donation to his boss's favorite charity only because his boss told him that he would be promoted if he donated and fired if he didn't. Does this donation show that the employee is morally good? Of course not, partly because he would have donated even if he despised the beneficiaries. This employee might have donated to that charity even without the boss's promises and threats, but that is hard to tell after the promises and threats are made. More generally, we cannot be sure who deserves moral credit when donations are forced.

The same goes for religious people. If they donate to charities after they have been promised Heaven for donating and threatened with Hell for failing to donate, then it is not clear whether they deserve moral credit for donating, because their motives are clouded. Probably most religious believers would donate to the same charities without the promises and threats, but which ones would do so is hard to tell once they believe in such extreme promises and threats.

Let me repeat: I am not saying that all religious people who help the needy are motivated by God's promises and threats. That claim would be wildly inaccurate. I doubt that many religious people have Heaven and Hell in mind when they help the needy. Most religious people give to charities because they want to help people in need. So do most atheists and agnostics. What is not clear, however, is how much of the statistical differences in charitable giving between secular and religious people can be explained by religious promises of Heaven and threats of Hell. To the extent that the difference in behavior is due to such self-interested motives, these differences show nothing about which group is morally better, much less "who really cares," as Brooks' title suggests.

Still, if religious people do in fact give more, isn't that good? After all, gifts to charity help the needy regardless of motive. People in need who are helped usually do not know or care whether their benefactors had purity of heart.

It is also not clear, however, that religious people really do donate more to charity than nonreligious people. Most of Brooks's evidence depends on self-reports.[46] He himself admits that "churchgoers [might] inflate their charitable giving in surveys . . . because of the perceived pressure to behave charitably as a person of faith."[47] That pressure alone might explain the differences reported in the surveys, even if there was no real difference in behavior at all. What benefits others is actual behavior, so we need some way to find out who really did donate to charity or help the needy. According to one standard review, "when we turn to studies that incorporate actual behavioral measures of helping, there is little evidence that religious people are more helpful than less religious or non-religious people."[48] This suggests that the self-reports on which Brooks relies so heavily are not reliable.

Brooks's categories also confuse the issue. He defines "religious people" as those who attend a religious service "nearly every week or more" and contrasts them with "secular people" defined as those who "attend infrequently (a couple of times a year) or never—or they say that they have no religion."[49] This definition of "secular people" oddly includes religious believers who attend church rarely. That misnomer distorts Brooks's results if religious believers who attend church less often also donate less to charity than religious believers who attend to church more regularly. That trend seems plausible if believers who attend less church are less socially inclined as well as less often reminded of charities and their importance. If rarely attending religious people are included within the category of "religious people" then the statistical differences between "religious people" and "secular people" might disappear. We don't know, so, without redefining his categories, Brooks cannot reach any justified conclusion about real atheists and agnostics.

Yet another serious flaw is Brooks's dismissal of political actions and donations. He insists that *"government spending is not charity."*[50] This restriction sounds plausible, but it distorts the issue. For one thing, voting to tax yourself more, such as on a school bond issue, is very much like contributing to charity, especially if you have no children in public schools. It is a conscious decision to try to make your money serve the needs of others. So is choosing to live in a state with high taxes to pay for social services that you personally do not use.

Moreover, strong religious belief is associated in the United States with conservative politics and skepticism about the role of government in solving economic problems. As a result, religious people are more likely to think that problems associated with poverty should be solved by private charities rather than by government programs. In contrast, secular people are more likely to think that it is the government's job to help needy people. They often add that it is more effective and fair for the government to provide needed services, because the burden of supporting private charities is not spread evenly and their resources are not reliable during economic downturns. Whether or not this "liberal" view is correct, those who believe it are more likely to focus on promoting government programs instead of private charities. Brooks himself admits this, in effect, when he says, "charity and conservative views on forced income redistribution go hand in hand."[51] This means that both sides try to help the needy, although they try in different ways. Neither side has a monopoly on beneficence, even if they have different views on how best to be beneficent.

Finally, we can repeat the lesson from earlier sections: correlation is not causation. Assume for the sake of argument that secular people do less for charity and religious people are motivated not by self-interest but by caring. Does this show that religion makes people better? No. As before, the causal train might run in the other direction. It seems plausible that people who do not want to spend their time or money working for charities will be less likely to attend church, where they are hounded and pressured to do what they do not want to do. Instead of religion increasing charity, it might just push out people who are less charitable.

In order to move beyond correlation to causation, psychologists manipulate variables. In one recent study,[52] twenty-six religious students (including twenty-four Christians) were compared with twenty-four other students (including nineteen atheists). All of the subjects were asked to unscramble sentences, but these sentences included religious words ("spirit," "divine," "God," "sacred," and "prophet") for only half of the subjects. These subjects were, thus, "primed" to think of

religious concepts. Both groups of subjects were then given ten
$1 coins and told that they could either keep all of these coins
or give some of them to another subject who had received
no coins and who would never learn their identity. Subjects
with religious priming gave $4.22 on average, whereas subjects
without religious priming gave only $1.84 on average. No sta-
tistically significant differences were found between religious
and nonreligious subjects. This result suggests that religious
priming increases giving among theists and atheists alike.

A follow-up study replicated the main effect in the general
public and added a twist. Some of the subjects were primed
not with religious concepts but with words referring to secular institutions of justice, such as "civic," "jury," "court,"
"police," and "contract." It turned out that this secular prime
had nearly as much effect as the religious prime ($4.44 with
the secular prime and $4.56 with the religious prime in con-
trast to $2.56 with neither prime).

This ingenious experiment finally supports a causal conclusion. Since religious priming affects giving, and church attendance involves repeated religious priming, this is probably
one mechanism by which church attendance increases charitable giving. This claim might seem sympathetic to theists.
However, religious belief is not what caused the giving, since
the effect occurred with atheists as well as theists. Church
attendance rather than religious belief is what matters on this
model. Moreover, atheists and agnostics can achieve the same
effect by priming secular moral concepts. This model, thus,
predicts that secular societies will not have significantly less
charitable giving if they make an effort to prime moral concepts, possibly by setting up communities that meet regularly
to discuss helping the needy.

Of course, more research is needed before any causal conclusion can be secure, and more work is needed by us all—atheists and agnostics as well as theists—to make more people more inclined to help the needy. Still, the emerging picture suggests that secular societies are far from doomed to selfishness, if they learn lessons from religious groups about how to make people more charitable.

OVERALLS

This chapter has barely scratched the surface. Our discussions of homicide, theft, abuse, cheating, discrimination, and charity have been too quick, incomplete, and inconclusive. Many moral topics and tons of empirical studies have not been mentioned. Still, I hope that some general themes have come out.

First, we don't know a lot. Most of the studies relating atheism or religion to immorality are flawed or limited in serious ways. Psychologists of religion have a lot more work to do.

Second, religious people have their virtues, and so do atheists and agnostics. If current studies are accurate, religious people are somewhat more charitable, but then secular people are less prejudiced. Neither side has a monopoly on virtue overall.

Third, the reported differences are between group averages. That means that any given atheist or agnostic might be extremely charitable, and any given religious individual might not be prejudiced at all. No study warrants any moral judgment about any particular individual based on whether he or she is religious or atheist or agnostic.

Fourth, these studies do not justify any claim that secular societies will descend into sleaze or that theistic societies will become authoritarian. The discovered differences are nowhere near dramatic enough for any generalization that crude.

Fifth, we can all improve by learning from each other. Atheists can learn from theists about how to induce charity. Theists can learn from atheists about how to become more tolerant. Plus, we can also all learn from each other about the morality we share.

What can we do with these lessons? One way to choose your worldview is practical: Choose your worldview by choosing which kind of person you want to be or which kind of people you want to live with. The empirical evidence outlined in this chapter can be helpful in making that choice.

It is crucial, however, not to confuse that practical choice with distinct intellectual issues. The fact that a worldview is statistically associated with a desirable kind of person or action does not show that the claims of that worldview are true. Such statistics do not show either that God exists or that God does not exist, for example.

A statistical or causal relation between religious belief and moral behavior also cannot show that "If God is dead, everything is permitted." The empirical evidence in this chapter addresses the very different question of whether "If *people believe that* God is dead, then *they are more likely to act as if they believe that* everything is permitted." In contrast, the claim that "If God is dead, everything is permitted" is about God rather than about belief in God. It is also about which acts are permitted rather than about which acts are done. Theists use this popular slogan to assert that nothing can be objectively morally wrong if God does not exist. The question, in short, is whether atheism entails nihilism, which is the denial of all real moral values, duties, and obligations. The next chapter answers that new question.

Chapter Four

WHAT'S WRONG?

So in everything, do to others what you would have them do to you, for this sums up the Law and the Prophets.

(Matthew 7:12)

How does morality matter? Let me count the ways. Morality separates us from lower animals. It also enables us to get along with other humans. Laws cannot replace morality without becoming oppressive. If most of us did not embrace morality, life for all of us would be "solitary, poor, nasty, brutish, and short," as Hobbes famously put it.[53] To live our lives, we need morality. To understand our lives, we need to understand morality.

On a more personal level, we all need to make choices, many of which involve moral considerations. We face temptations to cheat on taxes or spouses, to break a promise that we regret making, to lie in order to gain an advantage in a competition, to strike out at someone who angers us, to ignore someone who needs us, and even to steal when we are needy ourselves. We do not always get to do what we want most, if we accept moral restrictions. Of course, our moral beliefs also lead us to take stands on large and controversial issues like abortion, the death penalty, preventive war, environmental damage, affirmative action, pornography, gay marriage, vegetarianism, and so on. Which stand we take on such moral issues affects how we vote in elections, which laws we support, and which groups we join.

Some people might believe that they can go through life without holding any moral position one way or the other on anything, but that can't work for long. We all eventually need to think about what is or is not immoral both for ourselves and for others. Thus, if atheism did undermine morality, it would make life much harder than it already is.

Of course, we all need to decide not only whether morality has force for us but also which kind of morality to adopt in our lives. The shape of morality is very different for religious believers than for atheists. Two visions of morality compete in contemporary society. On one view, morality consists in obeying God's commands. On the other view, morality is independent of God and religion. Morality instead concerns harms to other people. These competing visions of morality lead to very different government policies, educational methods, medical practices, and ways of life. They lead to opposing stands on, for example, abortion, gay marriage, teaching evolution, prayer in schools, and displaying the Ten Commandments in courthouses. Even the words of the Pledge of Allegiance are disputed on moral grounds based in religious views.

Sometimes the influence of religion is hidden. At one conference that I attended, scientists spelled out many wonderful prospects for medical advances from stem cell research, and they also showed the need to use stem cells from embryos instead of other sources. Then a few speakers argued against embryonic stem cell research on openly religious grounds. Nobody knew quite what to say in response. How can you argue with religious dogma? It seemed like an easy case to me, but I worried that I was missing some secular objections. So I asked one speaker who had been on a government commission that had heard over a hundred witnesses for and against restrictions on embryonic stem cell research. He reported that not one single witness had spoken against such stem cell research other than witnesses who were there specifically to represent openly religious groups. This answer confirmed my view that there were no nonreligious reasons against embryonic stem cell research. Yet our government was restricting this useful research by limiting funding in response to organized religious groups. "Doesn't that conflict with our Constitution's clauses on religion?" I asked. The speaker's answer was clear, "Yes." But that did not stop the government policy or its religious advocates.

I suspect that part of the reason religious views of morality have such prominence is that contrasting secular views are fragmented and disputed. Another reason is that religious views are allowed to continue without careful criticism. In order to get straight on these important and divisive issues, then, we need to understand these two competing visions of morality and of its relation to religion.

My goal in the next two chapters is to explore the philosophical basis for these two views—starting with the secular view and then turning to the religious view in the following chapter. The issue here is not empirical, so I will not cite scientific studies or historical examples. The issue is also not about religious belief or practice. Instead, our new question is about God and whether God's existence is necessary for the existence of objective moral values and wrongness.

Many theists claim that God is necessary for objective morality, so atheism implies nihilism or, at least, the denial of objective morality. The next two chapters together argue for the opposite conclusion: Morality does not depend on God. Moral wrongness can exist without God.

My opponents in these coming chapters are not just evangelicals. Many other kinds of Christians as well as many other religions also hold that morality depends on God.

Nonetheless, many religions advocate pretty much the same moral prohibitions as my secular account, so what I say here will probably seem very familiar. I hope so. My goal is not to be strikingly original. The point is only to show that this core of morality can be articulated without relying on God or on anything that is peculiar to any particular religion or to religion in general. Hence, there is no need to accept any religion or to believe in God in order to accept and understand basic morality.

As always, my arguments will not persuade all readers. Nonetheless, I do hope to instigate further dialogue, to increase understanding of the secular position, to reduce fear of atheists and agnostics, and to make immoderate religious believers less confident and self-righteous.

The first step on this journey is to see how atheists and agnostics understand morality without God. This step is surprisingly short and simple.

HARM-BASED MORALITY

Consider rape. Rape is immoral. I hope you agree. Everyone I know—whether theist or atheist or agnostic—agrees that rape is morally wrong. Even most rapists admit that rape is immoral, although they do it anyway. Good arguments need to start from common ground that both theists and secularists can agree on. Hence, this moral judgment is a good place to start.

The question is not *whether* rape is immoral, but *why* it is immoral. On the secular view, the answer is simple: Rape is wrong because it harms the victim for no adequate reason. The victim feels pain and fear, loses freedom and control, is subordinated and humiliated, and suffers in many other ways. These harms are extreme and long lasting. They are not justified by any benefits to anyone, even if the rapist gains some minor and sordid pleasure. That is all it takes to explain what makes rape wrong, although much more could be added, as we will see.

What about rape without harm? Imagine that a woman is raped by her doctor while lying unconscious in her private hospital room, and she never finds out. That act is immoral as well, but there is no harm—is there? Yes, there is harm in this case, too. Harms include more than just pain. Loss of ability and control are also harms, and the doctor causes his victim to lose her ability to control what happens to her body in a very intimate way. He also violated her dignity and her rights, and such violations can count as harms. In all of these ways, he did harm her, even if she never found out. Furthermore, the doctor at the very least created a great danger, since his victim might find out that she was raped, and then she would suffer pain and humiliation. Significant risk of serious harm is enough to make this doctor's act immoral, even if it caused no actual harm.

This simple account applies as well to other kinds of immorality. Why is it morally wrong to kill other people? Because it harms them by depriving them of life. Why is it morally wrong to hit, kick, stab, or shoot other people? Because it harms them by causing pain. Why is it morally wrong to kidnap children? Because it harms them by terrifying them and taking away their freedom to go where they want. Why is it morally wrong to blind people? Because it harms them by taking away their ability to see. Why is it morally wrong to steal money from neighbors? Because it harms them by reducing their ability to buy what they want. Why is it morally wrong to break promises to friends? Because this may make them feel hurt, lose trust, become less friendly, and suffer lost opportunites, such as when they fail to arrange for someone else to help them because they thought that you were going to help them. Why is it morally wrong to lie? Because lies can undermine trust and mislead people into doing what harms them. And so on. All of these kinds of immorality are tied to harm of one kind or another in one way or another.

Of course, this simple story raises many questions. I cannot answer them all here. But I will say a few brief words about some of the main issues.

HARMS

First, what are harms? Most people agree that harms include death, pain, and disability. Disability includes loss of freedom and maybe also false beliefs insofar as false beliefs make people unable to achieve goals. Just imagine trying to buy a car when you believe that cars are sold at grocery stores.

Of course, these harms sometimes bring benefits in their wake. Death can end pain. Pain and disability can build character. Nonetheless, these harms are bad at least when they bring no benefit. Indeed, they seem bad to some extent even when their disvalue is overridden by the greater value of certain resulting benefits.

The argument here is not that almost everyone agrees that death, pain, and disability are harms and bad, so they are. Much less am I saying that agreement is what makes them bad. That argument would be just as silly as saying that most people believe in miracles, so there must be miracles. The case of miracles is different, simply because miracles conflict with scientific observation and theories, so we have plenty of reasons to doubt that miracles occur. In contrast, there is no reason to doubt that death, pain, and disability are bad. The belief that they are bad coheres with our other beliefs about what is rational and moral (as we will see). Then, in the absence of any reason to doubt, and in the presence of coherence among beliefs, the fact that so many smart people agree after thorough reflection provides strong reason to believe that death, pain, and disability are bad. It is still possible that everyone is mistaken. However, if you and I also agree with all of them, and if our beliefs are coherent, so we have no reason to deny what seems obvious, then we are justified in believing that death, pain, and disability are bad.

Despite these agreements, there are also many disagreements about what counts as a harm and about what counts as causing harm as well as about which harms are worse. Does boredom count as pain or harm? Do authors harm their readers when they write boring books? Are bad tastes harmful? Do restaurants harm their customers when they serve dishes that their clients dislike? On a larger scale, are women harmed by not being allowed to enter male bathrooms or to join male fraternities? Do drivers of large SUVs harm other people by sticking out of parking places or by contributing to global warming? Many questions like these are difficult to answer confidently, and any answer will produce disagreements. Nonetheless, these disagreements should not hide the fact that we agree on a lot. Almost everyone agrees that death, pain, and disability are bad. That is enough for the minimal account that I am trying to outline here.

What makes these harms bad? That is another tough question that I do not need to answer here. It is enough for my argument that these harms are bad, even if it is not clear what makes them bad or what it means to call them bad. Still, if you demand a general account of why these harms are bad, my colleague Bernard Gert plausibly identifies something as bad when it would be irrational to seek it (or not to avoid it) without an adequate reason.[54] Pain, disability, and death are bad on this account, because anyone who seeks them (or does not avoid them) without an adequate reason is irrational to that extent. Just imagine someone who seeks pain when that pain would not bring any benefits—it would not prevent any pain, disability, or death for anyone or bring any pleasure or ability to anyone. Even masochists seek pain because it gives them pleasure, often sexual. People who cut or burn themselves usually think that this will relieve the guilt or self-loathing that they would otherwise feel. These cases, thus, do not undermine the point that you would have to be really crazy to seek pain for its own sake without any other reason whatsoever. The same goes for death. People often seek death to avoid the horrible pain and indignities of a terminal disease or to gain glory and freedom for their homeland. Some religious people, such as suicide bombers, might seek death to further a political cause and also to gain access to Heaven at the same time. However, someone who wanted to die just for the sake of dying and for no gain to anyone at all would be really crazy—that is, irrational in a strong sense.

This answer leads to another question: What is irrationality? No answer can avoid controversy, but one sign that an act is irrational is that you would never advise anyone you care about to do it. Just imagine that your child told you that she is going to kill herself. You ask, "Why?" She says that she has no reason at all, she just wants to die. Would you advise her to go ahead? Of course not. That shows that you consider the act irrational. The same story would apply if she said that she was going to blind herself or cause severe pain to herself for no benefit to anyone. You would never advise her to do acts like these, either. To call such acts irrational is, then, at least partly, to say that you and other normal people would never advise your friends (or anyone you care about) to do them. Indeed, you would advise your friends not to do such acts.

This little theory reveals more about what counts as harm. Suppose your son says that he wants to play Russian roulette with one bullet in the chamber of a six-shooter. He does not want to die, but he does want to cause a risk of death to himself. Why? For no reason at all. You would advise him not to do this, I assume, so it is also irrational to cause a significant risk of death to oneself without a reason. That means that such risks of harm also count as harms.

Next, suppose that your son has a disease such that he will become paralyzed if he does not take his medicine. He has no reason not to take the medicine, because it is free, tasteless, and lacking in side effects, but he says that he does not want to prevent his paralysis. Here he does not cause the paralysis. The disease does that. But you still would advise him to take his medicine, I assume. Why? Because it is irrational for him to fail to prevent the harm, even if he does not cause that harm himself. Since failure to prevent a loss is just as irrational as causing that loss, a loss of ability or life also counts as a harm.

We might be able add to this list of harms. Maybe some items on this list are more controversial than I have suggested. Certainly each item needs to be specified more precisely. Still, the general shape of the list is pretty secure, I hope. So let's move on.

FROM SELF TO OTHERS

In the examples so far, a person causes harm to herself. There is nothing immoral about that. Causing harm to oneself without an adequate reason is irrational, not immoral. If I really want to cause pain to myself for no reason at all, you may call me crazy. If you care about me, you would probably advise me not to do it. However, it would be inaccurate and misleading to call such acts immoral.

Morality enters the story when harm is caused not (or not only) to oneself but to other people. Causing pain, disability, or death to others for no adequate reason is immoral. Why? The basic answer is that we have no reason to claim any special moral status for ourselves.

Suppose someone walks up and hits you on the nose. You ask why he did that. He says, "No reason. I just felt like it." You would think that his hitting you was morally wrong. Wouldn't you? You might not think this if he said that he saw a deadly stinging insect on your nose and he needed to kill it in order to save your life. You might also withhold adverse judgment if he said that his hand hit your nose only because he had an epileptic seizure or he fell when someone tripped him. Still, if he has no such justification or excuse, and if he admits it, then you would confidently believe that he did you wrong.

Now suppose that *you* are the one who hit *him* for no good reason. If it was wrong for him to hit you, wouldn't it also be wrong for you to hit him? We are imagining, of course, that you have no excuse or justification for hitting him. You hit him only because you feel like it. Moreover, you also have no special moral status. Morality protects him no more and no less than it protects you. He has exactly the same moral rights not to be hit as you have. He also has exactly the same rights to hit you as you have to hit him. Or, at least, you have no reason to claim any more rights than he does. Thus, if it is morally wrong for him to hit you for no reason, it is also morally wrong for you to hit him for no reason.

Next put it all together: It is morally wrong for him to hit you for no reason. If that is morally wrong, then it is also morally wrong for you to hit him for no reason. Therefore, it is morally wrong for you to hit him for no reason.

Will this argument convince everyone? Of course not. Arguments in morality never convince everyone. But it *should* convince everyone. The only way around this conclusion is either: (a) to admit that everyone in the world is allowed to hit you on the nose whenever he or she feels like it or (b) to claim that you are allowed to hit others when they are not allowed to hit you. Response (a) is abhorrent. Response (b) is arbitrary. Some people might not care about being hit or about being arbitrary. Nonetheless, their lack of concern need not stop us from criticizing them. Anyone who denies this conclusion is, thus, subject to criticism. That is enough for the argument to justify morality.

It might sound as if this little argument simply applies the Golden Rule. It does not. In fact, the Golden Rule is not so golden when you look at it carefully. *Matthew* 7:12 says, "do to others what you would have them do to you." Well, I would have men (and women!) give me a million dollars. Does that mean that I should or must give them a million dollars? Of course not. Sometimes the Golden Rule is formulated negatively: "Do *not* do unto others what you would *not* have them to do to you." That version is not much better. A judge who sentences a criminal to jail would not want the criminal to sentence him (the judge) to jail. Does that mean that the judge should (or must) not sentence the criminal? That would be absurd.

Defenders of the Golden Rule will accuse me of misinterpreting it. The judge has a reason to sentence the criminal, since the criminal committed a crime, whereas the criminal has no reason to sentence the judge, assuming that the judge committed no crime. But notice that the judge still would not *want* to be sentenced even if the judge did commit a crime. What matters to the moral status of imprisonment is not what the judge or the criminal *wants* but rather whether there is an adequate *reason* to cause the harm of imprisonment. That is what my little account of morality says. If it is also what the Golden Rule really means, then my only complaint is that the Bible and other religious texts misstate what the Golden Rule really means. What really makes certain acts immoral is not what I or anyone wants but, instead, that such acts cause harm to other people for no good enough reason.

Religion has clearly helped many people see or appreciate the force of the considerations behind my argument. Something like the Golden Rule can be found in many religious texts from a wide variety of religious traditions. Followers of those traditions usually interpret it in commonsensical ways rather than in the way that makes judges look bad and sadomasochists look good. Religious believers sometimes infer that religion should get credit for the moral insight behind the Golden Rule and that atheists will be morally hindered because atheists cannot rest their views on the Golden Rule. Much the opposite, however, the fact that the Golden Rule is stated in so many diverse religious traditions shows the insights behind the Golden Rule do not really depend on any religious tradition in particular. Those moral insights are part of common sense. Every religion needs to reflect this common sense in order to grow and survive for long. Religions also need to recognize the value of families. That does not show that religion gets credit for families. Hunter-gatherers had families long before they had anything like today's religious beliefs, such as evangelical Christianity. Analogously, the Golden Rule depends on a basic moral insight that was crucial to society regardless of religion. Hence, secular harm-based morality is not dependent on any particular religious tradition or on religion in general.

EXTENSIONS

Secular harm-based morality can be extended to many other kinds of acts. Suppose you duck, so the person who was trying to hit you in the nose misses you entirely, and you are not hurt at all. No harm done! Nonetheless, you would, I imagine, still think that it was morally wrong for the aggressor to *try* to hit you. One reason is that he might have hit you, so he caused a risk of harm to you. (Recall that it is irrational to risk harm to yourself even if the gun does not fire in Russian Roulette.) But suppose he is very slow, and you are very quick, so there is no significant chance that he will hit you. You would still judge that his failed attempt was morally wrong. And you still have no more moral rights than he does. Hence, it would also be morally wrong for you to try to hit him, even if you missed.

Some acts that are immoral do not cause harm directly by themselves, but they still indirectly bring harms in their wake. Suppose you tell me a secret about a past indiscretion when you were young, and I promise not to tell anyone. Despite my promise, I go ahead and reveal your secret to a mutual friend. This friend thinks nothing of it and soon forgets, so my act of breaking this promise does not seem to harm you directly. Nonetheless, I created a risk that our mutual friend would tell your secret to others. Even if our friend tells nobody else but only tells you that I had told your secret to him, then you would probably suffer disappointment, anger, and maybe fear that the secret would spread. You also would be unable to trust me as you had before, and our friendship would be undermined. Revealing secrets is a risky business, even when you get away with it. Moreover, by telling your secret to our friend, I reduced your ability to control who knows your secret, and this disability is a kind of harm. In these and other ways, then, breaking promises has at least indirect connections to harm, and that is what makes it morally wrong.

Promises also play a different role in harm-based morality. If I promise to drive you to the airport at a certain time, but I never show up, so you miss your plane, then I caused you harm, because I am responsible for your loss. In contrast, suppose we are roommates, and you expect me to get home at the time when you need a ride just because I usually get home then, but I never promised to come home at that time. Then, if you miss your flight, I am not responsible, and I did not cause the harm. In this way, my promise affects whether my act counts as causing a harm.

The notion of causation also shows how harm-based morality can incorporate special duties and obligations, such as duties to family and maybe sometimes country. Imagine that a child is not educated, so she suffers a loss of ability and opportunity in her future life. Her parents failed to educate her, but so did their neighbors as well as strangers on the other side of the world. Who is responsible for the harm to this girl? Her parents are the cause of that harm, because she is their child, not the child of neighbors or strangers. In this way, special relations can determine who is the cause of a harm and, thus, whose act violates harm-based morality.

This does not mean that we have no obligations to strangers. As we saw when discussing irrationality, it is also irrational to fail to prevent serious harm to oneself for no adequate reason. The lesson for morality is that we also should not fail to prevent important harms to others when we have no adequate reason not to prevent those harms. A common example is a baby who crawls into a pool and starts to drown. If I can save this baby's life at no cost other than my getting wet, which is not an adequate reason to let the baby die, then it would be immoral for me to walk away and let it drown.

Maybe I shouldn't save it when somehow I know that it will grow up to become a mass murderer. Maybe I don't have to save it when other people can and will save it if I don't. Maybe I have an excuse when saving it would be dangerous or when there are too many drowning babies for me to save them all. Moral theorists and common folk disagree about how far anyone needs to go to prevent harm to others. It is not controversial, however, that we should prevent a serious harm to another nearby person when nobody else can prevent it and we can easily and safely prevent it with no significant cost to anyone.

This does not mean that we must always do everything that we can to minimize the amount of harm in the world. That would require too much. We do not have to give to CARE every time we receive a request. Nor are we morally required to volunteer at every soup kitchen. To fulfill that unlimited demand, we would all have to spend our entire lives helping the needy. Still, we ought to do something. It is often hard to tell how much is too much to demand, and when we should or must help a particular person or group in need. Nonetheless, although the limits are controversial, it should not be controversial that we do have at least some positive duties to help the needy and to educate the ignorant in order to prevent the same old harms of death, pain, and disability.

Overall, there are many different kinds of immoral acts and many different ways for immoral acts to be related to harm, but what makes them all immoral is some relation to harm to others for no adequate reason. Those harms occur and those acts cause them regardless of whether the agent or the victim believes in God, and also regardless of whether there is a God. Hence, this harm-based morality is completely secular.

WHAT'S SO SPECIAL ABOUT YOU?

Theists often object that secular moralities cannot explain why humans are special. Other animals can also suffer and cause death, pain, and disability. Moreover, if humans evolved from ancestor species, as did other current species, then there is no hard and fast line between humans and other species or, at least, between humans and their ancestral species. There are only incremental differences along a continuum. However, morality is peculiar to humans. When male lions have forcible sex with female lions, those acts are not immoral. When humans do analogous acts, they are immoral. If harm to the victim is what makes rape immoral, then why isn't it also immoral when a male lion causes pain by having forced sex with a female lion? We need an explanation of this moral difference. Religions can explain this by saying that humans are chosen by God for a special role in the cosmic drama. What can atheists say?

Simple: humans are moral agents, because they are free and have free will. This freedom does not mean that human acts and wills are not caused. Instead, the only kind of freedom needed or useful here involves the ability to reflect on and respond to reasons. Partly by means of language, humans are able to reflect on the reasons for or against their choices in many cases (though not all). They often try to act according to those reasons, and they also often succeed (though not always).

Lions are not free in this way. Lions follow their instincts rather than reflecting on their choices. That is why you can lure an escaped lion back into its cage with a piece of meat on a string, but it usually takes much trickier traps to catch an escaped convict. Moreover, lions cannot judge their own acts or the acts of others, as far as we know, by thinking about morality. Their actions are not determined by any conception of what is moral or not. That explains why moral rules and principles do not apply to lower animals any more than they apply to avalanches that kill people.

In contrast, humans do have the ability to know what is right and wrong, again only usually. This point is recognized in the story of the Garden of Eden (*Genesis* 2–3) where eating the apple from the tree of the knowledge of good and evil was what set humans apart from other animals. Because normal adult humans have the ability to tell what is moral and immoral, and because they also have the ability to reflect on their choices and conform to what they take to be moral, they are governed as well as protected by morality—or, in other words, they have moral duties in addition to moral rights. In this respect, humans are special, even according to secular morality.

Indeed, humans are special in pretty much the way that theists themselves claim. Many religions present free will and knowledge of good and evil as the distinguishing mark that shows why humans are made in God's image and are his favorite species. This religious gloss is unnecessary. You don't need to add that humans were made in God's image or that we are His favorite species or anything religious. The reason we have moral duties is simply because of our special abilities that even atheists and agnostics can recognize.

This point also answers a common conundrum. If intelligent but bloodthirsty Martians descended onto Earth and began killing humans, how could we convince them that killing us is morally wrong? Theists could proclaim to the

Martians that we humans are endowed by God with special moral rights, but what could a secular moralist say to the Martians? Atheists and agnostics could repeat the same argument as above. Since the Martians are intelligent, they should recognize that we are able to formulate and follow moral rules and principles. Then, if we harmed them for no adequate reason, they would see their rights as violated and our acts as wrong. But they have no reason to ascribe moral rights to themselves and moral duties to us without granting those same rights to us and moral duties to themselves.

Of course, this abstract reasoning will not stop blood-thirsty Martians, but then neither will a declaration that we have rights from God. If we could somehow convince the Martians that God will punish them if they kill us, that might work; but how could we convince them of that? In any case, the secular argument that I outlined above will give them a moral reason not to harm us, even if they do not care about that reason. There are some situations that mere reasoning cannot get you out of, but that does not show that the reasoning is faulty. The fault lies in those nasty Martians, who won't listen to good reasons.

EXCEPT

It is time to explain the perpetual exception clause: "... unless you have an adequate reason." It is obviously not always wrong to harm other people. Judges and police cause harm when they jail criminals. Doctors cause harm when they amputate limbs. But those harms are caused in order to prevent greater harm in the future. That is why these acts are not immoral.

It is still true that these kinds of acts are morally wrong in other cases where they cause harm for no adequate reason.

In addition to the degree of harm, consent also affects whether a reason is adequate. Boxers cause lots of harm to their opponents, but that need not be immoral if valid consent was given. However, criminal sentencing shows that actual consent is not always necessary. It is also not clear that consent is sufficient to justify harm. In Germany recently, a cannibal was convicted for killing and eating someone who consented on videotape to be killed and eaten. Consent in such cases might be invalid if it is based on a mental illness, so the victim is incompetent to give consent under that condition. Then the fact that he actually consented is not adequate to justify causing him death. There was a heated dispute in Germany about whether his consent was valid and whether it did justify the cannibal's actions.

Many other moral disagreements also concern when reasons are adequate to justify harm and who should not be harmed. Is the fact that someone committed murder in the past an adequate reason to kill that person even if killing him will bring no further benefits in the future? Is "[an] eye for [an] eye" (*Exodus* 21:24) an adequate reason? Many disagreements in morality are also about non-moral facts, such as whether affirmative action will harm the groups that it is trying to help. These disagreements are intriguing. That is why they fill debates and classes in ethics. Still, our fascination with these disagreements should not hide the underlying agreement that it is morally wrong to cause harm in the many cases where no normal informed person sees any reason as adequate.

Some empirical evidence of near-universal agreement comes from the Moral Sense Test Web site at Harvard University run by Marc Hauser, Fiery Cushman, and Liane Young.[55] They and their colleagues have accumulated responses to various moral dilemmas by over 200,000 people from more than one hundred countries. There is surprising agreement on some of their cases. Consider, for example, the side track case, where a runaway trolley will kill five people on the main track unless Denise pulls a lever to turn the trolley onto a side track where it will kill only one person. Around 90 percent agree that it is permissible (that is, not morally wrong) for Denise to pull the lever. This response is not affected much by religion, culture, gender, or any of the other demographic factors that they explored. There is, thus, consistent agreement that saving five lives in this way is an adequate reason to do what will knowingly lead to someone else's death. The agreement would, presumably, be even higher if there were 100 people on the main track and/or if there were only a flower, a dog, or a murderer on the side track. I also hope that almost everyone would agree that it would be morally wrong for Denise to pull the lever if there were ten people on the side track and only five on the main track. If so, there is near-universal agreement that saving five lives is not an adequate reason to cause ten deaths. Most people forget about cases like these because they are so obvious and boring. Still, a fair assessment of what counts as an adequate reason to cause harm should not forget such clear cases. Indeed, it should be based on them.

Another major source of disagreement is scope. The general principle that it is immoral to cause harm for no adequate reason does not say *whom* it is wrong to cause harm to. The group to whom it is wrong to cause harm can be called the *protected class*. In earlier times, some people denied that women and slaves were in the protected class. Thankfully, those debates are over, but other scope questions remain: Are animals, including chimpanzees and chickens, in this protected class? Are fetuses at any stage of development protected? What about patients in persistent vegetative states? What about future generations? What about Martians, if there are any? I mention these controversies not to resolve them. It would be foolish to try to settle such issues here. I need not solve all moral problems in order to show that many moral judgments can be based on my harm account.

It is enough that many cases are clear. People almost always admit that others who are like them in whatever ways they see as relevant are also in the protected class. It should not be surprising that adult white men think that other adult white men are in the protected class, women think that other women are in the protected class, and slaves presumably thought that they should be protected as well. This tendency suggests that a failure to include all rational humans in the protected class is due to a failure of impartiality or else a misunderstanding of those other people. Besides, all the readers of this book, I hope, will agree that all rational humans—including women and slaves as well as citizens of foreign countries and believers in other religions—should be seen as falling in the protected class. It is just as wrong to harm them as any other person.

The crucial point here is that this commonsensical view of morality has no need of God. Harmful acts can be immoral on this basis even if God does not exist, simply because these harmful acts would still hurt other people even if God did not exist. Some harms are worse than others, and that can sometimes be used to determine which reasons are adequate to justify causing which harms, even if God does not exist or never tells us which harms are worse. And we can cite human abilities to explain why we have moral duties that other animals lack, even if we are not special in any God's eyes. This harm-based account of morality is totally secular. As a result, it can be accepted by atheists, by agnostics, by believers in non-Christian religions, and even by evangelical Christians (although they might deny that this is all there is to morality, as we will see). That acceptability across the board is one of its advantages.

OBJECTIVITY

This account also makes morality objective. If what makes an aggressive war morally wrong is that it hurts innocent people, then whether it is wrong does not depend on my desires, such as whether I want to harm those people. It also does not depend on my beliefs, such as whether I believe that the war will hurt those people. (A reasonable mistake might excuse it, and overriding benefits might justify it, but harmful acts like wars are still presumptively wrong insofar as they need to be excused or justified.) Thus, atheists and agnostics can hold not only that there are moral facts but also that these moral facts are objective rather than subjective.

In contrast, many theists claim instead that what makes rape immoral is only that rape violates God's command. This alternative account makes morality less objective than on the harm-based account. On the divine command theory (which will be discussed in the following chapter), what is morally wrong depends on God, so moral wrongness is objective only in the weaker sense that whether an act is morally wrong does not depend on whether *we humans* think that it is morally wrong. On that divine command theory, moral wrongness is not objective in the stronger sense that whether an act is morally wrong does not depend on whether *anyone* thinks that it is morally wrong. Its wrongness does, after all, depend on what one person—namely, God—thinks, wills, or commands. There is no such dependence on the secular harm-based view of morality, where moral wrongness is objective even in the stronger sense that whether an act is morally wrong does not depend on whether *anyone* (including God) thinks that it is morally wrong. Thus, the harm-based account makes morality more objective than the theistic theory.

This point might seem surprising, because theists often say that, without God, morality must be subjective. Not so. Some atheists and agnostics are relativists, conventionalists, constructivists, non-cognitivists, and even nihilists. However, their position on morality need not be shared by all atheists. What atheists agree on is that God does not exist. They need not (and do not) agree on the abstruse question of whether morality is objective. Anyway, whether or not other atheists agree, I myself disavow subjectivism, relativism, egoism, nihilism, conventionalism, non-cognitivism, and postmodernism. I do believe in moral truth, moral universals, and some kinds of moral knowledge. The little discussion in this chapter tells you roughly why.

Of course, this harm-based account of morality is not conclusive and needs to be developed. What if it were shown to be inadequate? There are many other secular alternatives ranging from contractualism to Kantianism and virtue theory. But suppose that all of those secular moral theories were inadequate. That would be a problem for atheism only if theists could give a better answer. They cannot. As we will see in Chapters Five through Seven, the alternative theistic theory of morality has much more serious problems of its own. Besides, even if we cannot say *why* it is immoral to cause unjustified harm to others, that should not make us doubt that it *is* immoral for moral agents to cause unjustified harm to others. Atheists can, thus, legitimately hold on to objective morality, even if nobody has a fully satisfying account of its ultimate basis.

FAMILY AND COUNTRY

Is my account complete? Not in this way: Many moral issues have not been discussed. But the question here is, instead, whether *all* immorality is harm-based. Even if some acts are immoral because they cause unjustified harm, other acts also seem immoral independently of harm. Jonathan Haidt has argued forcefully that "liberal" harm-based morality includes only part of what counts as morality according to many people, especially non-Western cultures and "conservatives" in the West.[56] The three main areas that harm-based morality is supposed to miss are hierarchy, loyalty, and purity.

Although Western moral codes tend to be individualistic, hierarchical social relations are central to many moral codes, even in the West. For example, parents have special obligations to children, and children have special duties to parents. I already responded to this objection in part when I pointed out that parents rather than neighbors are the cause of harm to a child when that child suffers from neglect. On the other side of life, if elderly parents suffer from neglect, because nobody visits them or helps them, their children's choices to spend their time and money elsewhere rather than caring for their parents can make those children the cause of harm to their parents. Other people—both acquaintances and strangers—also fail to visit or help those elderly parents, but these other people are not the cause of the harm if they have no special relation to those elderly people. Moreover, the parents are harmed more when their own children do not visit or help them in old age, if only because they would usually prefer to see their own children rather than a stranger. The same points apply, of course, to siblings and other family members in need. Thus, it is not hard for harm-based accounts of morality to incorporate special obligations to families.

The same goes for obedience to authority. When a child disobeys a parent, this disobedience creates family problems. Even when the child's disobedience causes no immediate harm, it fuels future tendencies to disobey on later occasions when disobedience will be harmful or at least risky. Every parent knows these dangers. Similar dangers can arise from disobedience to most laws.

In addition, loyalty to your family, company, or country can help that group run smoothly and thereby avoid the harms that result when that group fails to run smoothly. Eastern moralities call this social harmony, but we can just as well call it avoiding harm. Social cohesion and feelings of social attachment are very important to many people, so losing them is harmful. There is no reason why harm-based morality cannot recognize and even emphasize social goods and harms like these.

This way of viewing loyalty and social relations might still strike some critics as missing something important. However, I am not suggesting that people should think only about avoiding harm when they visit their elderly parents or join patriotic celebrations. I also admit that disagreements remain about what exactly is morally right or wrong in tricky situations. Nonetheless, the secular harm-based account is able to explain why disloyalty and disrespect for legitimate authorities is normally immoral.

Harm-based accounts can also explain the limits of these areas of morality. Loyalty to an in-group goes too far when it turns into social exclusion. Why? Because the people who are excluded get harmed, often very badly, and also because the in-group itself could benefit from those who are excluded. Similarly, respect for authority goes too far when it leads to blind obedience. Why? Because blind obedience harms rather than helps the group to which one is loyal. When parents order their children to engage in immoral acts or unwanted sex, it is not immoral for these children to disobey. When employers order their workers to engage in immoral acts, such as by skirting safety regulations, it is not immoral for these employees to disobey. And when governments order their citizens to fight unjust wars, it is also not immoral for these citizens to disobey. Citizens might owe a certain degree of deference to the judgment of governments, who often (though not always) have better information. However, when citizens have strong enough reasons to distrust the government and also strong enough reasons to believe that obedience would be too harmful, then disobedience might be true patriotism. We would probably disagree about particular examples, but what matters here is only the general point: The limits of loyalty and authority are determined by harm, so this area of morality causes no trouble for the secular harm-based view.

SEX

Real trouble seems to arise for a harm-based account if any immorality is harmless. Then that account covers only part of morality, not all of it.

Most proposed examples of harmless immorality concern sex. The Bible and traditional religions condemn masturbation as immoral. Some even say that masturbators are bound for Hell. Why? Usually the reason is that masturbation is dirty or unnatural. It is obviously not unnatural in the sense that it violates laws of nature, like the law of gravity. If it violated laws of nature, nobody could do it; but they do. Masturbation might be unnatural in the sense that it is artificial, at least in some cases. However, being artificial would not make it immoral. There is nothing immoral about artificial flowers. Instead, the best argument against masturbation claims that our sex organs have a natural function or purpose, which is to reproduce, and masturbation uses those sex organs apart from or contrary to that natural function or purpose.

The situation is not so simple, however, because sex organs have more than one function. The extensive nerve endings in our sex organs are there for the purpose of giving pleasure. That is why we evolved to have so many nerve endings in that location. Thus, masturbators use those organs—the nerve endings—for the purpose that they evolved (or were designed?) to serve. In this respect, masturbation is natural even in the sense that refers to purpose or function.

Moreover, even if masturbation did not serve the natural purpose of our bodily organs, it is not always immoral to use our organs for new purposes. It was not immoral for Houdini to untie knots with his toes during his magic tricks.

What about using bodily organs *contrary* to their natural purpose or function? It is dangerous to use your teeth to open a bottle, because they were not made for that purpose. Granted—I do not advise opening bottles with your teeth. But why not? Because it risks breaking your teeth, which will hurt a lot and make it harder to chew food. Again, we are back to harm. In the old days, some moralists claimed that masturbation was harmful, because it supposedly made masturbators unable to resist temptation or to enjoy normal reproductive sex. Today, however, experts report that masturbation is extremely common, and there is little, if any, reason to predict that masturbation will cause harm. Even if it did, it would probably cause harm only to masturbators themselves, so it would be only irrational and not immoral. But imagine that somehow masturbation caused harm to others, such as by breaking up a marriage or by causing serious loss of self-control that left masturbators unable to resist cheating in harmful ways. That still would not spell trouble for my harm-based account of morality, because then what made masturbation immoral would just be the harm that it caused to others.

Why am I talking about masturbation at all? It is not a pressing moral issue in our culture. One point is to show how arbitrary and weird moral prohibitions become if they are based on what is "unnatural" rather than on what is harmful.

A more pressing issue in our culture is homosexuality. Many theists object to homosexuality because it is unnatural. But if that is supposed to be enough to make homosexuality immoral, then they have to infer that masturbation is also immoral on the same grounds. (Indeed, the same grounds would also make it immoral to have heterosexual sex while using birth control or after menopause.) I just argued that those grounds don't work in the case of masturbation. Thus, merely being unnatural also cannot be enough by itself to show that homosexuality is immoral.

Theists might respond in several ways. First, they might say that homosexuality is dirty or impure or disgusting or repugnant. However, homosexuals do not find it so, and neither do I. Homosexual sex can be an expression of true love. True love is not disgusting. It is beautiful. Moreover, what is disgusting or repugnant (to some) need not be immoral. Just think about touching vomit, if you don't mind. That's disgusting, but not immoral.

Many opponents of homosexuality argue, instead, that the "homosexual lifestyle" is unhealthy. There might be something to this (although many of my friends might be shocked to hear me say so), but only if we are talking about the wild lifestyles that these critics have in mind. Many homosexuals do engage in lifestyles that are far from ideal for them and for others. Of course, heterosexuals do so, too. And many homosexuals have long-lasting love-filled relationships. So do many heterosexuals. It is not being homosexual or heterosexual that makes a relationship moral or immoral. Instead, it is being loving, stable, and healthy. Why? Because unloving, unstable, and unhealthy relationships are harmful to the people in them. Just ask those people themselves. Again, it all comes back to harm as the basis for morality. When sex is a harmless expression of true love, whether heterosexual or homosexual, then what's the problem?

What about harm to so-called traditional family values? I value many aspects of traditional families (especially my own!), and it would be immoral to undermine the ability of people to form such families when and how they want. Still, nobody has ever explained how stable loving homosexual relationships take away anybody else's ability to live the way he or she wants with whatever family values he or she wants. Public recognition of homosexual marriages is another matter, which I will not address, because it would take us too far off topic. The point here is only that homosexual love and its expression in homosexual sex need not cause harm of any sort that would make it immoral.

Sometimes evangelicals retort, "What if everybody did that?" Here, "If everybody were homosexual, nobody would have children, and the human species would die out, so nobody should be homosexual." The form of this argument is common but faulty. Just ask yourself: What if everyone chose not to have children? Then the species really would die out. Does that mean that it is immoral for anyone to choose not to have children? Is it morally obligatory to have children? Of course not. The problem arises only if everyone actually makes that choice, but they won't. Similarly for homosexuality: Even if there would be problems if everyone had homosexual sex, that would not show anything wrong with homosexuality, because only a minority want to have homosexual sex. Instead of asking, "What if everyone did that?" we should ask, "What if everyone were *allowed* to do that?" If everyone were allowed to have homosexual sex, there would be no problem. Besides, even if everyone were exclusively homosexual, that would not destroy the species. Homosexuals can have children, if only the laws would let them. They cannot have children with their life partners, but they can use artificial insemination, and many do.

Of course, some theists still might respond by quoting the Bible:

> Do not lie with a man as one lies with a woman; that is detestable. (*Leviticus* 18:22)

> If a man lies with a man as one lies with a woman, both of them have done what is detestable. They must be put to death; their blood will be on their own heads. (*Leviticus* 20:13)

> Because of this, God gave them over to shameful lusts. Even their women exchanged natural relations for unnatural ones. In the same way the men also abandoned natural relations with women and were inflamed with lust for one another. Men committed indecent acts with other men, and received in themselves the due penalty for their perversion. (*Romans* 1:26–27)

I will argue in Chapters Five through Seven that such divine commands, even if they are divine, are no basis for moral judgments. But then such biblical passages pose no threat to my secular harm-based account of morality.

It is not always so clear, however, whether a moral belief depends on religious assumptions. Many religious thinkers go out of their way to deny that their moral prohibitions on harmless acts depend on religion. They often refer instead to "natural law." In some cases, that label is just a hidden way of referring to a religious basis. If the reason we ought to follow "natural law" is only that God laid down that law, or if what makes something "unnatural" is only that it violates God's plan for nature, then the real basis of natural law is religious after all. That religious basis is not accepted by atheists, agnostics, and followers of other religions, so they need not worry about that kind of natural law. In contrast, if "natural law" really refers to something natural as opposed to supernatural, then naturalistic atheists and agnostics might be able to accept it. I will not survey the many versions of natural law theory here. All I need to say is that atheists can accept natural law if it really is natural, but they can reject it as dubious if it turns out to be supernatural. Either way, natural law theories cannot create any real trouble for atheism or agnosticism.

Religion-based prohibitions cannot be used against my secular harm-based theory because I am not trying to give an account of everything that anyone thinks is immoral. That would be pointless and impossible, because people disagree so much. I am only trying to suggest an account of what makes acts immoral when they really are immoral. If my account does not imply that a certain act—such as homosexual sodomy—is immoral, that feature is no problem at all for my theory unless that act really is immoral.

What about weirder kinds of "harmless immorality"? Incest between consenting adult siblings (with no offspring or regrets), necrophilia (with prior permission), and cannibalism (without killing) might be examples in some very, very special circumstances. Such acts seem immoral, and, although they are almost always harmful or at least dangerous, we might be able to imagine unusual circumstances where these acts cause no harm to anyone. If they really are immoral even in those odd cases where they are harmless, then my harm-based account of morality is not complete.

There's that pesky little word "if" again. These acts do strike me, like most people, as immoral. But maybe this is just because these acts are disgusting and inadvisable, rather than immoral. Or it might be because these acts always create risks of harm, even when no actual harm occurs. I am not certain. Are you? How can you be sure? After all, our moral intuitions arose in normal situations to deal with common acts, not with such strange cases, so it is not clear that our moral intuitions are reliable in this peculiar arena.

Anyway, if my harm-based moral theory is incomplete, so be it. It still reveals what makes almost all common immoral acts immoral. It also shows that much of morality has nothing essentially to do with God. Call that harm-based core of morality "shared morality," because it is shared with theists, who agree that rape, murder, theft, child abuse and neglect, and so on are morally wrong. There might be a few additional moral prohibitions that are not harm-based, possibly including prohibitions on all incest, necrophilia, and cannibalism, and these might be justified without reference to either harm or religion. Call this part "extra morality." Yet another class of moral beliefs cannot be justified without religious backing. Call them "religious morality."

My goal is not to provide an account of extra morality. Nor do I need to deny all extra morality. After all, even if some extra morality is based neither on harm nor on religion, that cannot support the slogan that "If God is dead, *everything* is permitted." Even without accounting for extra morality, a harm-based account of shared morality is enough to show that at least *some* (indeed, many) acts are not permitted even if God is dead.

My goal is also not to provide an account of religious morality. I want to argue against religious morality. If a moral prohibition depends on religious belief, so that it cannot be justified apart from religious belief, then I and other atheists would reject it. I would also oppose anyone enforcing it on other people who do not share that religious belief, because such prohibitions are so often abused and harmful. My secular harm-based account of morality does not support religious morality as accepted by other people, but so what? That is a feature rather than a bug of my account.

Some theists might still have a sense that atheists and agnostics are missing something important. A community needs to share a common moral code in order to function properly and for its members to feel connected to each other. Some theists have a strong sense that a harm-based morality is just too thin to support society. There is something to this: How would you like it if your neighbors repeatedly and openly practiced incest, necrophilia, or cannibalism, even if only when those acts were truly harmless? This would make many people very uncomfortable, and that matters to social cohesion and trust. However, discomfort is a kind of harm, and social breakdown and distrust cause still more harms, so harm-based morality can accommodate these points. Besides, as far as I know, there has thankfully not been any great rush to commit incest, necrophilia, or cannibalism. Even people who deny that these acts are immoral in extremely unusual circumstances do not go out and do them. Murder, rape, theft, fraud, and domestic abuse are much more common. The serious problems for our societies lie in causing harm to others.

Of course, some opponents might claim that atheism is the first step down the slippery slope to harmless immorality and the next step is to harmful immorality. One step leads to the next inevitably, they fear. This claim about how beliefs lead to actions is a prediction that is subject to empirical evidence. You cannot decide this question by looking deep into your own soul, since the question is about other people as well as yourself, and all of us are partial on such issues. The only reliable way to tell whether secular harm-based morality really does lead to harmful actions, and whether it is enough for communities to thrive, is to observe impartially the actual behaviors and conditions of secular individuals and societies. We discussed some evidence in Chapters Two and Three. What matters in the present chapter is only that, if (another big "if" that I deny) a secular harm-based account of morality really did lead people to cause harm to others, then it would be immoral by its own lights, or at least spreading the word about it would be presumptively immoral. It still might be true. It still might capture the immorality of what really is immoral. That is enough for this chapter.

OBJECTIONS

This completes my positive argument for a secular harm-based account of morality. I have not, of course, come anywhere near to resolving all moral problems. Indeed, I have not resolved any controversial moral problem. That was not my aim. I actually doubt that we can resolve many difficult moral issues, so we need to learn humility in the face of basic moral questions. But I have not argued for that either. My only goal has been to show how atheists and agnostics can provide an initial rough outline of the beginning of an objective account of the shared part of morality without invoking God.

Many questions remain, of course, and they lead to objections. I will try to answer the main objections in the remaining chapters.

First, even if my secular theory works fine, is there a religious alternative? The most common religious account of morality is a divine command theory. If that theory provides a better foundation for morality, then my secular view is in trouble. I will criticize that alternative so as to respond to this objection in Chapter Five.

Second, even if my secular theory tells us what is immoral, does it give us enough reason to be moral? Some theists charge that secular moralists have no adequate answer to the perennial question, "Why be moral?" If so, that would be a major gap in the secular harm-based account. I will respond to this objection in Chapter Six.

Third, how can we figure out what is morally wrong or right in difficult cases? Religious moralists can look to revelation and prayer. How can secular moralists make tough decisions? Without an answer to this question, the secular harm-based account might not be of much practical use. Chapter Seven will respond to this objection.

Each of these objections captures one of the main ways in which theists claim that morality depends on God or on religious beliefs and traditions. In responding to these objections, I will, in effect, be completing my demonstration of how morality works just fine without either God or religion.

Chapter Five

WHAT'S SO DIVINE ABOUT COMMANDS?

So Joshua defeated the whole land...; he left none remaining, but destroyed all that breathed, as the Lord God of Israel commanded.

(*Joshua* 10:40)

Theists often assert that atheists can't really believe in objective morality. These theists are not talking about what is psychologically possible. Their claim is that a certain combination of views is incoherent and indefensible. They think that objective moral values, facts, or truths could not exist if God did not exist; so, if I really followed out the implications of my views on God, then I would have to give up my views on morality in Chapter Four and, instead, become a moral nihilist or subjectivist.

In support of this charge, theists often cite our old foe, "If God is dead, everything is permitted." But why believe this?

Just because Nietzsche or Ivan Karamazov said it? Theists think that Nietzsche and Ivan are wrong about almost everything else, so why agree with them on this point? Theists might be suggesting that since Nietzsche and Ivan are atheists, all other atheists must agree with them. "Atheists think this, and you are an atheist, so you must believe it, too." That's silly. Atheists do not have to agree with everything that other atheists say. Atheism does not have any creed or catechism that all atheists must accept on pain of expulsion (from what?). Atheists agree that God does not exist. Beyond that, atheists disagree about all sorts of things, so you can't legitimately hold all atheists responsible for a mistake by some atheists.

Most atheists today, myself included, believe in evolution. Theists often claim that evolution undermines objective morality because evolution implies that morality evolves, so evolution excludes any universal, absolute, or objective morality. This argument misunderstands evolution. What evolves are species and their traits. Humans evolved to have less hair and also to be better at physics and mathematics than their ancestors. That does not suggest in any way that the laws of physics and mathematics evolved. Although we as a species evolved so as to be able to discover and appreciate the laws of physics and mathematics, the laws themselves were the same in the day of the dinosaurs: $2 + 2 = 4$ and $E = MC^2$ were both true when T Rex ruled.

Morality is like physics and mathematics in this respect (though not in many other respects, of course). What evolves are only moral *beliefs* and *attitudes*, not moral *facts* or *truths*. When T Rex ruled, there were no free agents to rape or be raped, but it was still true that free agents ought not to rape other free agents. This moral principle can be true even at

times when it does not apply to anyone because nobody
could break it. After all, rape is wrong even for people who
are alone on inescapable islands or who are quadriplegics so
they could not rape anyone. The moral prohibition on father-
daughter rape does not have exceptions for fathers who have
no daughters and are now sterile, or even for women who
cannot be fathers. Rape can't be wrong for some people but
not for other people. The fact that a moral prohibition cannot
be broken, so it does not apply to a particular case, does not
make it false in that case. Hence, it is not all that odd to say
that moral prohibitions held even before there were humans
who could violate them.

At later times, many of our human ancestors did not
believe that slavery and marital rape were immoral, but it
was *true* that slavery and marital rape were morally wrong,
even in those dark days of the past. The reason should be
obvious by now: Slavery and rape caused harm to victims
who were people, so they were protected by the same moral
rules as everyone else. These victims had moral rights even if
most people at the time did not recognize their rights.

In other cases, which acts cause harm and, hence, which
acts are morally wrong do change, simply because the circumstances change. In modern Western societies, it is harmful to fail to teach your children to read and write, but this was
not harmful in the Middle Ages, when most people did not
need to read or write. Nonetheless, these cases are different
from slavery and rape, because slavery and rape *were* harmful even during times when they were not seen as immoral.
Hence, the fact that circumstances change—so some acts that
did not cause harm in the past do cause harm now—does
not at all undermine my point that other acts that did cause

harm without any adequate reason were immoral. They were immoral even at times when people failed to recognize their immorality.

Thus, the basic moral law against causing harm without an adequate reason does not change any more than the basic laws of mathematics and physics. This constancy follows from the objectivity of morality on the secular harm-based account and is completely compatible with the evolution of human moral beliefs and attitudes. Evolution properly understood, then, is no problem for atheists and agnostics who believe in objective morality.

The only remaining reason for thinking that atheism implies nihilism is that morality depends on commands by God. Many theists accept such a divine command theory of morality. If it is true, then atheists who do not believe in God also should not believe in morality or, at least, in objective morality. This view deserves a chapter of its own, because it is central to the outlook of so many respectable theists, including most evangelical Christians, and because it presents the main religious alternative to my secular harm-based morality. In this chapter, I will try to show why this position falls apart.

WHAT IS THE DIVINE COMMAND THEORY?

A divine command theory of morality claims that what makes immoral acts immoral is that God commanded us not to do them. Some versions refer, instead, to God's will instead of explicit commands, but that variation will not matter here. Besides, if God's will is never revealed to us in a command, then it is hard to see how it could be fair to hold us responsible for acting contrary to His will. Hence, I will focus on theories that base morality on God's commands, not just His will.

It is crucial to distinguish this divine command theory from the claim that God wants us not to harm each other, so He commands us not to harm others, unless, of course, we have an adequate reason. That "God cares" view would be compatible with a harm-based account of what makes acts immoral.

The divine command theory is also distinct from the view that we come to know what is morally wrong or right by seeing what God commands, because He knows best which acts cause harm to others without an adequate reason. That "God knows" view is also compatible with my position that harm is what makes those acts immoral.

In contrast with these other religious accounts, the divine command theory claims that God's commands *constitute* moral wrongness as well as moral duties, obligations, and rights. Constitution is a very strong relation that reveals not just which acts are morally wrong but what makes them morally wrong. We might, for example, tell whether a liquid is water by how it looks and tastes, but what makes it water is its chemical composition—H_2O. Analogously, according to the divine command theory, God's command not just a way of discovering what is morally wrong. It is the very essence of moral wrongness.

This relation of constitution implies universal generalizations in both directions. All water is H_2O, and all H_2O is water. Similarly, if God commands us to do something, then it is our moral duty to do it, whatever it is. If God commands us not to do something, then it is our moral duty not to do that, whatever it is. And if God does not command us either to do it or not to do it, then it is morally neutral in the sense that we do not have a moral duty either to do it or not to do it, again whatever it is. In short, divine commands are both sufficient and necessary for moral duties.

This strong divine command theory of morality is common among evangelical Christians. It is also useful for our conversation here, because it provides a clear foil to my secular harm-based account. Consider rape, again. According to the harm-based account, what makes rape morally wrong is roughly the harm it causes. According to the divine command account, what makes rape wrong is that God commanded us not to rape. The contrast could hardly be more stark. Moreover, if the divine command theory were true, it would follow that, "If God is dead, everything is permitted." If there is no God to command us, and if all moral wrongness were constituted by God's commands, then no acts would be morally wrong.

This conclusion follows because the standard divine command theory is about *all* moral duties, rights, and wrongness. Every moral duty is supposed to be constituted by a divine command. A partial divine command theory could, in contrast, claim that only some moral duties are based on divine commands.[57] Rape and murder, for example, might be immoral because of the harm they cause, whereas failure to pray or keep the Sabbath holy might be immoral because of God's commands. This partial divine command theory might be easier to defend, but it is not relevant here. Without universality, the divine command theory would not imply "If God is dead, *everything* is permitted." If even part of morality is not based on divine commands, then that part of morality keeps *some* acts from being permitted even if God is dead. Hence, this partial divine command theory would not conflict with the harm-based theory of at least part of morality. That is why I will focus here on the divine command theory as a theory of all of morality.

WHY BELIEVE IT?

Although many evangelical Christians and other theists advocate a divine command theory, it is hard to find any reason to espouse it. It is not entailed by any biblical passage. It is hard to imagine that God revealed it in a prayer or a religious experience. So, why should anyone accept it?

The best argument—because it is the only argument—is that "Moral laws presume a moral lawgiver."[58] This quip might seem to spell trouble for a secular account of morality. Even if a harm-based account shows that it is morally *bad* to hit others, it still might fail to capture moral law, duty, obligation, and wrongness. For real obligations, duties, and wrongness, these theists argue, someone must have the authority to issue laws and then to hold people responsible. That's where God comes in. Only God has the authority to issue moral laws and to hold people morally responsible, so God is required for any moral law to exist. And if God is necessary for moral laws, then He is also necessary for moral duties, obligations, and wrongness. So they say.

It is not clear why an authority is supposed to be necessary for moral wrongness. After all, there is something logically wrong about contradicting yourself. There is something epistemically wrong about believing in life on Mars for no reason at all. And there is something rationally wrong about causing oneself severe pain for no reason (recall Chapter

Four). No specific person or God issued these laws of logic, epistemology, or rationality. Thus, there do seem to be several kinds of wrongness that do not depend on any specific lawgiver. If we get moral wrongness out of the harm-based account without God, why isn't this enough?

Those kinds of wrongness involve violations of general rules, which could be called laws, such as laws of logic, of epistemology, and of rationality. There are also natural laws without a lawgiver. What makes them laws is that they hold in counterfactual situations: The law of gravity would hold even if the particles of the universe were arranged in very different patterns. These laws of nature are not normative, but the basic laws of logic, epistemology, and rationality, which are normative, also hold in counterfactual situations: Hasty generalization would be a fallacy even if it were committed on another planet. This is the basis for calling them laws. But then there do seem to be laws without any lawgiver in a variety of cases.

Still, let's assume for the sake of argument that moral laws, duties, and wrongness do require something with the authority to hold people responsible. God cannot play that role for atheists, so what can? Why not other humans? We each have the authority to hold people responsible for violating moral duties. If my neighbor steals jewelry from his grandmother, then surely I have the authority to criticize him and his action (even if he is let off on a legal technicality). You do, too. You and I do not have the authority to put him in jail or to send him to eternal torment, but all that shows is that moral sanctions take other forms. Morality is enforced verbally by public condemnation or socially by ostracizing violators. If you think those sanctions are too little, just imagine how you would react if someone publicly denounced you as a thief (or even just a liar) and then refused to have anything to do with you. That could be a death sentence in hunter-gatherer times, and it is very disagreeable even today. Moreover, we all have the authority to vote for representatives who enforce moral norms through formal institutions, such as by legal punishments. Much criminal law and some tort law enforces morality. We collectively have the authority to impose such sanctions. Thus, there are plenty of authorities—you and me and other humans—to enforce moral obligations, if any such authority is needed.

Dictators might seem to create problems for this account, if dictators cannot be punished legally, criticized openly, or ostracized. It might be useful to make sure that dictators believe in God, so that they will believe that someone above them will hold them responsible if they violate morality. However, this objection confuses actual punishment with liability to punishment. People who act immorally often do not in fact get punished. That's a fact of life. Nonetheless, they are *liable* to punishment. If another human were to criticize or punish them, then they would have no legitimate complaint. That was the point above. Such liability to punishment is enough to ground moral wrongness and moral duties, even without actual punishment.

Some readers will not be satisfied. They want a guarantee that everyone who acts immorally will be punished. You cannot get that guarantee without God. But the demand for that guarantee is unreasonable. There are few guarantees in this world, and we all have to learn to live without them. If you postulate a supernatural power to guarantee whatever you hope will happen, then you will end up believing all kinds of nonsense. The fact that such postulation leads to absurdity when it is generalized shows that we should not always require such a guarantee. It might seem reasonable to you in the case of a Christian God, but this cannot be used as an argument against atheism.

Another source of dissatisfaction might be the need for a lawgiver in addition to a law enforcer. Even if other people have enough authority to hold people responsible, they do not make the rules in morality. If they did, morality would not be objective in the strong sense (defined in Chapter Four).

Now the question is why we should assume that moral wrongness requires any specific person who is the lawgiver. You can refer to "the moral law," but that is misleading. Moral wrongness is what really needs to be explained, and there is no more need for a lawgiver in order to explain moral wrongness than there is to explain the wrong answer on a math test, the wrong conclusion to an argument, the wrong belief about life on Mars, the wrong investment in the stock market, or the wrong move in chess. As we saw above, lots of rules can be called laws without a lawgiver. Hence, atheists can admit that there are moral laws, but only in a sense that does not require a lawgiver.

The problem here is that "moral law" is only a metaphor. Moral rules are like government laws in some ways. They are normative generalizations that restrict actions by people on the basis of their relations to other people. However, that does not mean that moral "laws" must share every feature with government laws. Government laws do require a lawgiver (normally, though not in the case of customary laws). Secular moral theorists can coherently claim that the metaphor breaks down at just this point: Moral laws do not require a lawgiver in the way that government laws do.

Besides, the notion of God as a moral lawgiver has its own problems. It is not only that God does not exist, or that God does not issue commands, or that, even if He did, we could not know what He commanded (see Chapter Seven). Even if God did exist and did issue known commands, why would you and I be morally required to obey them? One common answer is that God will punish us if we disobey Him. That would give us a strong self-interested reason to obey, but that reason would hardly be a moral duty. I might have a self-interested reason to obey the commands of a tyrant who will punish me if I disobey, but I still do not have any moral duty to obey that tyrant. Another common answer is that we owe God gratitude for creating us. However, although children should also be grateful to their parents for creating them, children do not have a moral obligation to do everything that their parents tell them to do. Yet another common answer is that God the father knows best, so, if God tells us that an act is morally wrong, it is. But how do we know that God is always correct? Unless we have some independent reason to believe that certain acts are morally wrong, we have no reason to believe that God is correct when He indicates to us through His commands that those acts are morally wrong. This answer, then, also cannot tell us why we morally must obey God's commands. Without any reason to accept that assumption, we have no reason to accept the divine command theory.

WHAT'S WRONG WITH DIVINE COMMANDS?

Even if a theory is not justified, it still might be true. This general point holds as well for the divine command theory.

Despite the lack of any good argument to support it, many people still seem to believe that morality is constituted by divine commands.

But think about it. The divine command theory says that what makes rape immoral is nothing more nor less than a divine command not to rape. That means that if God had not commanded us not to rape, then there would be nothing immoral about rape. Absurd! The victim would still have been harmed just as much, and there would still be no adequate reason to justify that harm. Hence, rape would still be immoral.

Let's go further. The divine command theory claims that it is immoral to disobey God's commands. Then, if God had commanded us positively *to* rape, then that command would have created a moral requirement for us *to* rape. More absurd! If God threatened to torture everyone eternally if I did not rape someone, this horrible consequence of refusing might perhaps create a moral obligation for me to rape; but then the basis of the moral obligation would be to prevent the harm to the others, not to obey the tyrannical command for its own sake. No command by any third party could by itself create a moral obligation to rape.

The problem, to mimic the theistic slogan, is that "If God's commands constitute morality, then everything is permitted." Since the *source* of the command rather than its *content* is what creates moral obligations on this view, moral obligations could have any content whatsoever, no matter how absurd or arbitrary.

This problem is not new, and several old responses are well known, but no response is adequate. Defenders of the divine command theory often reply that God never would or could command us to rape. But how do they know this? After all, God commanded Abraham to kill his son, Isaac (*Genesis* 22:2). (Abraham did not kill Isaac in the end, but he did commit attempted murder, and he also had a moral obligation to kill Isaac during the time before God rescinded His command, according to the divine command theory.) God also commanded the Israelites to destroy "all that breathed" in an entire country (*Joshua* 10:40; compare 11:20), and this time the command was reportedly carried out. So, how can we be sure that commanding rape is beyond the pale for God?

The common retort is that God is all-good, and rape is bad, so God would or could never command rape. But murder is also bad, so what about God's commands to Abraham and Joshua? Besides, this argument assumes that rape is bad on independent grounds. We need those independent grounds in order to know that God would not command it. But this just admits that not all moral standards depend on divine commands after all.

Admittedly, this standard says only that rape is bad, not that it is wrong. Hence, theists could try to escape by saying that God commands us not to rape, because rape is bad on independent grounds. These grounds might even be harm-based. Still, they insist, rape does not become morally *wrong* until God commands it.

Wrongness is, admittedly, distinct from badness. Nonetheless, this response falls flat. Because rape is so bad in a moral way, it would be bad for God to command us to rape. It would also be bad for Him not to command us not to rape. The badness of rape, thus, puts moral constraints on God's commands. But then it seems that we would not have any moral duty to obey such bad commands, even if God issued those bad commands. It also seems that we would have a moral duty to do what He should have commanded even if He did not actually command it. Our moral duties, then, do not really depend on what God *does* command. They depend on what He *should* command, and that in turn depends on which acts are bad enough. So our moral duties, as well as moral obligations and wrongness, end up depending on harm rather than on divine commands after all.

These objections might seem too tricky because they ask about the moral implications if God were to do something that God could not do by His very nature. It's like asking what my pet cat would look like if she were a fish. Similarly, defenders of the divine command theory often claim that it makes no sense to ask whether rape would be wrong if God commanded us to rape or failed to command us not to rape, because it is not possible for God to do such things.

There are technical ways to handle counterfactuals with necessarily false antecedents, but this topic is way too difficult to go into here.[59] Still, we can think about the opposing counterfactuals: If God commanded us to rape, then rape would still be morally wrong. And if God did not command us not to rape, then rape would still be morally wrong. That's what secular moralists want to say, and it sure seems plausible to most people, regardless of any technical details about counterfactuals with impossible antecedents.

The point can also be brought out by considering other religions. Imagine a religion that postulates a god (named Bacchus Goldstein) who, by its very nature, commands everyone to drink wine every day but never to eat pork. Can we reasonably ask what our moral obligations would be if there were no god who issued those commands? Sure. Can we reasonably ask what our moral obligations would be if that god did exist but did not issue those commands? Yes, again. We would be asking about a situation where there is a god close enough to be identified as the same god but whose nature differs enough that he did not care about wine or pork. My cat is essentially feline, but it still makes sense to say that, if my cat were a fish, she would have gills and fins instead of lungs and legs. Similarly, we can say that, if Bacchus Goldstein did exist but did not care about wine or pork, and if all morality depends on commands of Bacchus Goldstein, then we would not have any moral obligations regarding wine or pork.

Of course, rape is not like wine or pork, because rape is immoral. That's the point. If the immorality of rape depended on God's commands, then it would be just like wine and pork in my example. The postulation of a God whose nature is to issue commands about wine and pork cannot make those commands any less arbitrary. Similarly, to postulate a God whose nature is to forbid rape cannot make that command any less arbitrary, unless there is an independent standard by which rape is immoral. So there must be such an independent moral standard.

The same point applies when Christians define God to be all-good, unlike Bacchus Goldstein. If all we knew was that God is all-good, but we did not know that rape is bad, then we would not know whether or not God could command rape. In order to get from the premise that God is all-good to the conclusion that God could never command us to rape, we need to assume that rape is bad and wrong. That suppressed premise requires an independent standard that makes rape bad and wrong. Divine command theorists cannot assume such a standard, because the whole point of divine command theory is to deny any such independent standard of moral wrongness. Hence, they cannot appeal to the wrongness of rape in order to show that God could never command rape. And if God could command rape, then the divine command theory yields implausible results. Either way, it is in trouble.

This dilemma is, of course, related to the problem suggested long ago by Socrates in Plato's dialogue, *Euthyphro*. That dialogue is about piety, but its basic point can be extended to show that divine command theories fall into a dilemma: Assume that God commanded me not to rape. Did God have any reason to command this? If not, then His command was arbitrary, and an arbitrary command can't make anything morally wrong. On the other hand, if God did have a reason to command us not to rape, then that reason is what makes rape morally wrong, and the command itself is superfluous. Hence, divine commands are either arbitrary or superfluous. Either way, morality cannot depend on God's commands.

Many theists try to fend off this standard objection by claiming that God could not command rape because his commands flow necessarily from his nature. That dogma does not solve the problem, however, both because commands that flow from a god's nature can still be arbitrary (as in the case of Bacchus Goldstein) and because, even if the Christian God is all-good by His very nature, we cannot know that He would not command rape unless we assume that rape is immoral for some independent reason. But if there is such an independent reason against rape, then that reason is what makes rape morally wrong, and the command itself is superfluous. So we are back in Euthyphro's dilemma. The divine command theory has no way out of this dilemma.

BUT THAT'S NOT ALL

The preceding dilemma might strike some readers as just a little too tricky (or confusing), so it is worth adding that the model of morality proposed by the divine command theory is implausible in more commonsense ways as well. I will quickly mention two more problems.

First, the divine command theory suggests that moral wrongness comes from a person who created you, is more intelligent than you, has power over you, issues commands, and punishes noncompliance. That makes morality a lot like family rules. The analogous position on family rules is that what makes it wrong for children to break family rules is simply that their parents issued those commands. The problem with this account should be obvious. Consider a small boy who thinks that what makes it morally wrong for him to hit his little sister is only that his parents told him not to hit her and they will punish him if he hits her. As a result, this little boy thinks that if his parents die, then there is nothing wrong with hitting his little sister. Maybe some little boys think this way, but surely we adults do not think that morality is like this. To see morality this way is, in a word, childish.

Indeed, to call the divine command theory childish is insulting to children. Older children know better. Larry Nucci[60] found that almost all Amish teenagers said that if God had not commanded them not to work on Sunday, then it would not be wrong to work on Sunday. In his terms, they saw this wrongness as conventional and dependent on authority. When asked why it is wrong to hit other people, many of these Amish teenagers replied that hitting is wrong because God commanded them not to be aggressive or violent. Luckily,

Nucci did not stop there. He went on to ask these same Amish teenagers whether it would still be morally wrong to hit other people, if God had made no rule against hitting other people. More than 80 percent of these Amish teenagers replied that hitting would still be immoral. In Nucci's terms, they treated the wrongness of hitting as moral rather than conventional (or authority dependent) even though they had talked about it as if it were conventional. Their responses, thus, show that even teenagers who were brought up in a strict religious way and who espouse the divine command theory still recognize that morality has a sound foundation outside of God's commands.

Second, the divine command theory also makes morality hard-hearted. Divine commands by their nature allow no exceptions for the sake of human welfare. If God commands us to kill nonbelievers, then, according to the divine command theory, it becomes morally wrong not to kill non-believers regardless of how much suffering obedience will cause to innocent people. God is supposed to have taken account of that suffering before He issued His command, so, if there were justified exceptions, God would have said so. Indeed, God often rules out exceptions explicitly:

> If your brother, the son of your mother, or your son, or your daughter, or the wife of your bosom, or your friend who is as your own soul, entices you secretly, saying, "Let us go and serve other gods," . . . you shall not yield to him or listen to him, nor shall your eye pity him, nor shall you spare him, nor shall you conceal him; but you shall kill him. (*Deuteronomy* 13:6–9; see also *Exodus* 22:20, *2 Chronicles* 15:13—So much for family values!)

...when the Lord your God has delivered them over to you and you have defeated them, then you must destroy them totally. Make no treaty with them, and show them no mercy. (*Deuteronomy* 7:2: see also 20:10–16 and *Joshua* 10:40 and 11:20—So much for the Geneva Conventions and just war theory!)

The lack of concern for human welfare is blatant.

Of course, modern Christians ignore these commands: They make treaties and do not kill unbelievers. We are grateful. Nonetheless, this defect of divine command theories continues to the present day. Consider contemporary religious opposition to research using embryonic stem cells. Almost nobody opposes embryonic stem cell research except on the basis of religious views. Those who do oppose embryonic stem cell research claim that it is morally wrong no matter how much good it would do. Even if embryonic stem cell research is needed to cure juvenile diabetes, to enable paraplegics and quadriplegics to walk again, and so on, as many doctors claim, it would still be morally wrong if what makes it wrong is simply that God commanded us not to do it. This view of morality has separated morality from human suffering by basing morality on commands coming from another world. Such a view is callous.

Many good Christians would reply that God commands us not to harm others and to help others in need. Those commands are not hard-hearted. Maybe not, but suppose that parents command their son to be nice to his little sister. Their son is then nice to his sister, but only because his parents ordered him to be nice to her. If they had not commanded him to be nice to his sister, then he would not be nice to her. This boy might not seem hard-hearted, but his motivations are far from ideal. Analogously, anyone who helps and refrains from harming others just because God commanded her to do so might not be hard-hearted, but her motivations are far from ideal. It would be better for them to help and refrain from harming other people out of concern for those other people.

That is what we ought to teach our children. Studies of development and education show that children develop better moral attitudes as adults if they are raised to empathize rather than to obey commands without any reasons other than to avoid punishment.[61] To raise children to obey God's commands just because God commanded them will undermine true caring and true morality.

Many Christians do, of course, help others because they care about those others. They are good people. Still, if that is their only motivation, then they are not really following the divine command theory. They are, instead, following a harm-based morality. Like the Amish teenagers, they do not let their religion undo their common sense here. That is wonderful, but it cannot save the divine command theory from the charge of being hard-hearted.

Of course, motivations might be mixed. Some Christians help the needy and avoid harming other people *both* because they care about those people *and also* because of God's commands. That's also fine, at least if their concern for those others is sufficient to motivate them to avoid and prevent harm even without God's command. But then, again, the divine command theory is not really necessary after all, so this case again cannot save the divine command theory from the charge of being hard-hearted.

The crucial cases are Christians who act morally solely because they take God to have commanded them to do so and, especially, those who would obey what they take to be God's commands even if they think that their acts will cause serious harm to innocent people without any compensating benefit to anyone. Those are the people who really follow the divine command theory, and they are hard-hearted, because concern for other humans plays no essential role in their actions. I doubt that many Christians really are like this, but that is because most real Christians, like the Amish teenagers, have more common sense than is built into the divine command theory.

This discussion is incomplete. All I have tried to do is present the basic ideas behind the divine command theory and some of its main problems. To complete our comparison of the secular harm-based theory with the divine command theory, we need to ask at least two additional questions. First, is there an adequate reason to be moral on either theory? Second, how can we know what is right or wrong according to either theory? These questions will occupy us in the next two chapters.

Chapter Six

WHY BE MORAL?

But the cowardly, the unbelieving, the vile, the murderers, the sexually immoral, those who practice magic arts, the idolaters and all liars—their place will be in the fiery lake of burning sulfur.

(Revelation 21:8)

Ouch! Burning sulfur! That sounds horrible, and it lasts forever, reportedly. All who are faced with a threat like that have very strong reasons to be moral—or, at least, to do as they are told. What reason to be moral could a secular morality possibly propose that could be as strong as a threat of eternal torment? And if a moral theory cannot provide an adequate reason to be moral, isn't that a serious deficiency?

SECULAR REASONS

Even without Hell, secular moralists can still give a variety of reasons to be moral. First, despite popular rumors, it is normally in our interest to be moral. Immorality rarely pays. Sure, some people get away with horrible misbehavior, but the odds are against them. When people cheat, steal, or kill, they take big chances. And even if they get away with it, they usually won't be happier, or much happier, than if they had made more modest gains honestly. They will often be hounded by guilt or fear of rivals or of punishment. The life of a crook is not really as sweet as it might seem or as cool as it is portrayed in some popular fiction. Thus, even if our only reasons were based on self-interest, we would still almost always have strong reasons to be moral.

But not always. Harming others is sometimes in some people's best interest, even considering probable costs. In those cases, some theists say that only a divine threat of Hell provides a reason to be moral. Since atheists and agnostics do not believe in God, they do not believe in divine retribution for sins, so they have to admit that sometimes some people could get away with immorality and then they have no self-interested reason to be moral. Does that mean that these people have no reason at all to be moral? No. That conclusion would follow only if every reason had to be self-interested, selfish, or egoistic. There is no basis for that assumption.

Many reasons are not based on self-interest. That should be common ground between theists and atheists. Despite what theists often assert or assume, there is no connection whatsoever between atheism and egoism. Atheists can recognize and act on nonegoistic reasons as much as anybody else can.

To understand how nonegoistic reasons work, we need to ask what a reason is. This abstract question is rarely asked, but its answer is simple: A reason is a fact with rational force. Its force can turn an otherwise irrational act into a rational act.[62]

For example, imagine that I pay someone to cut into my abdomen with a sharp knife, knowing that this will cause me intense pain. Also imagine, if you can, that I have no reason to do this. Maybe I have a desire to be scarred or to feel pain, but fulfilling that desire gains no benefit for me or for anyone else. This act seems irrational. Anyone who does this needs psychiatric help. I assume that you agree. If not, substitute your own example of an irrational act.

A fact that turns this act from irrational to rational is then a reason. What kind of fact does that? Suppose that I pay a doctor to cut into my abdomen with a sharp scalpel in order to remove my kidney because it is diseased and will kill me if it is not removed. In this new situation, it is no longer irrational but is, instead, rational for me to pay this doctor to cut into my abdomen, even knowing that this will cause me intense pain. The fact that paying this doctor to cut into me is necessary to save my life turns an otherwise irrational act into a rational act. Thus, the fact that this act prevents my own death is a reason (and, indeed, an adequate reason) for me to do this act.

This reason is self-interested. What about other people? The same account of reasons applies again. Just imagine that I am paying the doctor to remove my kidney so that it can be transplanted into my spouse, who will die without my kidney. Again, it is no longer irrational but is, instead, rational for me to pay the doctor to cut into my abdomen, knowing that this will cause me intense pain (even with anesthesia). The fact that paying this doctor to cut into me is necessary to save my spouse's life again turns an otherwise irrational act into a rational act. Hence, the fact that this act prevents this other person's death is a reason (and, again, an adequate reason) for me to do it.

Nothing essential changes if the transplant recipient is a stranger. Suppose I hear about someone who will die without a kidney, so I decide to pay a doctor to remove my kidney and transplant it into the stranger, who consents. Maybe not many people would do this, but those who contribute organs are not being irrational, so the fact that this act saves a stranger's life is a reason (and an adequate reason) to do it.

One more variation: Instead of being the donor, imagine that I am the one who needs a kidney transplant. If a suitable kidney is available from a corpse of someone who consented before dying, then it would be irrational for me to decline to pay the doctor to cut my abdomen and transplant that kidney, assuming that I had no reason not to use this kidney (such as that it might be defective or someone else needs it). In contrast, imagine that I can take a kidney from a live patient in a neighboring hospital room with no risk to myself, but that patient did not consent to donate a kidney. Now it is no longer irrational for me to refuse to take that kidney. If taking the kidney would harm someone else without consent, then I would not be crazy to refrain from taking it. If I do refrain, then I will not be refraining for no reason at all. The harm to that person is, thus, a reason for me not to take that kidney, even if taking it posed no risk to me personally. And, again, this reason is adequate to make what I do rational.

Cases like these show why and how harms to others provide reasons for me. The fact that an act prevents harm to another person can be a reason for me to do that act. The fact that an act causes harm to another person can be a reason for me not to do that act. These facts are reasons, even if the other people are strangers. Crucially, these reasons are not self-interested. They are facts about the interests of other people, not me.

These unselfish reasons can answer the question, "Why be moral?" On my harm-based account, what makes an act immoral is that it causes harm or fails to prevent harm to others. The question "Why be moral?" then asks what reason I have to avoid harming others or to prevent harm to others. My answer should be obvious by now: The fact that an act causes harm to others is a reason not to do that act, and the fact that an act prevents harm to others is a reason to do that act. There is, then, always a reason to be moral on this secular account. And often these reasons are adequate, because they are strong enough to make it rational (or not irrational) to be moral.

To return to our paradigm of immorality, what reason do I have not to rape? My main reason is not that my act will hurt *me*. It is that rape hurts the *victim*—the person who is raped. That reason is enough to show that it is not irrational for me to refrain from rape, even if I wanted to rape, and even if rape were in my own self-interest. Because it harms the victim, I would not be crazy to refrain from doing it. If I choose not to do it because it would harm the victim, then I will not be choosing for no reason at all. In this way, avoiding or preventing harm to others is a reason for me.

Of course, some rapists might not care about harming others. They are rapists, after all. However, all that shows is that they lack motivation to be moral. Motives are crucially different from reasons. Even if rapists lack motivation not to harm their victims, there is still a reason for them not to harm their victims, because it would not be irrational or crazy for them to refrain from harming those other people simply in order to avoid harming other people. A harm-based account thus shows that there is a *reason* for them to be moral, even if it takes something else—such as good character or training—to *motivate* them to be moral.

Although reasons are distinct from motives, they often go together. The secular harm-based reason to be moral can motivate people to be moral as long as they care about other people. Almost all atheists and agnostics *do* care about other people, just as theists do. Theists sometimes talk about atheists as if they are all selfish egotists, but that is inaccurate (as we saw in Chapters Two and Three). Without that faulty assumption, there is no basis for claiming either that atheists and agnostics have no reason to be moral or that they are not motivated to be moral.

Nonetheless, some people still wish for a reason that is strong enough to motivate *everyone* to be moral and also to make it *always* irrational to be immoral. I doubt that secular moral theories can establish that strong kind of reason to be moral. For people who really do not care about others, the solution is found in retraining or restraining rather than in theory.

Is this limitation a problem for secular accounts of morality? I doubt that, too. If we demand this extreme kind of reason to be moral, then we are bound to be disappointed. The solution to our disappointment is to give up this demand, not to imagine a higher power that we want to fulfill an illegitimate demand. Besides, this limit on secular theories would be a problem only if the alternative religious account could provide a better reason to be moral. It can't. That is what I will show in the next section.

RELIGIOUS REASONS

What reason can religious moralists give to be moral? Hell, they've got lots of reasons. Eternal bliss for being moral, and eternal damnation for not being moral. In some religions, such as in Judaism, there is no Hell of this kind. Many Christians also do not believe in Hell. But, if there are Heaven and Hell, what more could you want?

We could want the right *kind* of reason. Imagine that the King of Curls threatens to kill all of his subjects who do not shave their heads on May 21, though there is nothing special about that date. Now all of his subjects have a reason to shave their heads, right? Yes, they have a reason of one kind. However, the command to shave their heads on that date is just as arbitrary as it was before. There is no reason to pick that date instead of another or to pick shaved heads instead of mohawks or shaved legs. When the reason to do something is based on force or threat, it need not bear any connection to the content of the command.

This point extends easily to reasons to be moral. Imagine a mother trying to teach her son not to hit his sister. The mother might try to convince her son that harm to his sister by itself is a reason for him not to hit her. Or the mother might just threaten to lock her son in the basement for a week (or a lifetime?) if he hits his sister. This threat will, indeed, give him a reason not to hit his sister. However, it will not give him the right kind of reason. It will not teach him to care about his sister.

Divine threats of Hell or promises of Heaven operate in the same way. If our only reason to be moral is to avoid Hell or get to Heaven, then our motivation is far from ideal. Even a total psychopath, who cares about nobody else, but who believes in Hell, would have this reason to be moral, but this reason would not give the psychopath any reason for the content of the moral restrictions themselves. The psychopath would still see moral restrictions as just as arbitrary as a law requiring him to shave his head on May 21.

Different audiences react to this point in different ways. Some people really want a reason to be moral that will motivate psychopaths, even if it is not connected to any reason why certain acts are immoral. They are rightly scared of psychopaths, so they want a reason that will convince psychopaths to be moral. Other people want a reason to be moral that does not leave morality arbitrary, because the reason to be moral shows why those moral acts are moral. They want a moral reason rather than a selfish reason. I share the latter goal, but I can appreciate the former wish. Unfortunately, I doubt that the former wish can be fulfilled. No reason will succeed in convincing everyone to be moral. This is another obvious but hard fact of life that we need to learn to live with.

Besides, religions do not really teach that all immorality will be punished. Theists sometimes assert that punishments and rewards are distributed perfectly according to desert:

> On the theistic view, God holds all persons accountable for their actions—evil and wrong will be punished and the righteous will be vindicated. Despite the inequities of this life, in the end the scales of God's justice will be balanced.[63]

However, as we saw, that is not what the Bible says:

> [E]very sin and blasphemy will be forgiven men, but the blasphemy against the Spirit will not be forgiven. (*Matthew* 12:31; see also *Mark* 3:28)

"Every" means that rapists (along with murderers and thieves) will be forgiven, if only they later turn to Christ and sincerely ask forgiveness. But then they are not punished after all.

Moreover, as we also saw, the Bible tells believers that God commands them to kill non-believers (*Deuteronomy* 13:6–9, quoted above; see also *Exodus* 22:20, *2 Chronicles* 15:13). Thus, the Bible suggests that killing nonbelievers is morally required rather than morally wrong. If so, and if you kill such a non-believer, you will not be punished. You might even be rewarded. However, it is actually morally wrong—not right—to kill another person just because that other person does not share your religion. I hope you agree! Hence, the Bible does not say that all people who do what really is immoral will be punished. What it says, instead, is that all people who disobey God will be punished.

Finally, the Bible is filled with stories, such as the Great Flood, where whole groups of people are punished for the sins of only some, even though many of those punished were too young to have been morally guilty of anything, much less anything bad enough to warrant a death penalty. (Abraham sees this as unjust: "...to kill the righteous with the wicked, treating the righteous and the wicked alike. Far be it from you! Will not the Judge of all the earth do right?" *Genesis* 18:25). Because of stories like that, the Bible cannot support the prediction that only wrongdoers will be punished or that the righteous will be vindicated. If innocent people get punished along with guilty ones, then such group punishment gives no incentive to avoid wrongdoing—although you should pick your friends wisely. Since many innocent people get punished, and many guilty people get forgiven, the Bible does not really give everyone a reason to be moral.

The divine command theory also undermines hope for a universal reason to be moral. Divine command theorists claim that acts are morally wrong only because those acts violate divine commands. Thus, people who do not and cannot know what God commands them to do also do not and cannot know which acts are morally wrong. However, when people have (and had) no way to tell whether their acts are wrong, even if those acts really are wrong, those people do not deserve to be punished. It is not their fault. That is common sense as well as common criminal law (in a standard version of the insanity defense). But then people who cannot know God's commands also cannot deserve to be punished. Assuming that God will not punish those who do not deserve to be punished, many wrongdoers who cannot know God's commands will not be punished after all.

To illustrate the point, consider a possible divine command not to sculpt statues of Jesus. People who had never heard that command could not know that it is morally wrong to sculpt statues of Jesus, so they should not be held morally responsible if they do sculpt statues of Jesus. God might build into them a natural aversion to sculpting statues of Jesus, but they still would not know that it is morally wrong, because they would have no idea what makes it morally wrong to sculpt statues of Jesus, and they would have no reason to believe that their aversion reflects moral wrongness if moral wrongness is constituted by divine commands.

Now compare horrible murderers who lived before Jesus and never had any access to a Bible or to Christian beliefs. There are plenty of examples, including Sulla, dictator of Rome; but pick your own favorite. If the divine command theory were correct, then the command not to murder would be like the command not to make statues of Jesus. But then these murderers could not know that it is morally wrong to murder, so they would not deserve to be punished. That's absurd. Of course, these murderers deserve to be punished, even if they had no access to any divine command. The reason is that these murderers could know that it is wrong to murder on the basis of the harm to their victims. If harm is the basis of moral wrongness, these murderers can know what is immoral and can justly be held responsible. But if the basis for moral wrongness really were divine commands, then these murderers could not know that murder is morally wrong, so they could not be justly held responsible or punished.

Divine command theorists usually reply at this point that God implanted in everyone a natural ability to see what is morally right or wrong. That is supposed to explain how our ancient murderers could know that their acts were wrong. Maybe so, but maybe not. How can we tell? In any case, this response really just admits the point. Ancient murderers as well as modern people like us know which acts are immoral by seeing the harms that acts cause, not by thinking about divine commands. They do know what is immoral but not in anything like the way that the divine command theory would suggest. In this respect, secular theories have a better explanation of how ancient murderers could deserve to be punished.

Moreover, although ancient murderers could know what was morally right and wrong, they still did not know about Heaven and Hell. Hence, if their reason to be moral was only that immorality would land them in Hell and morality would get them to Heaven, then these ancient murderers could not know of any reason to be moral. In contrast, they did have a reason to be moral and they could know it, if the fact that their acts caused harm to others was a reason for them to be moral, as secular accounts claim. In this respect, secular theories have a better explanation of how ancient murderers could become aware of a reason to be moral.

Finally, what about modern atheists and agnostics? Do they have any reason to be moral, according to religious views? That depends on who goes to Heaven and Hell. On one view, Heaven is a reward for freely chosen good works, and Hell is a punishment for freely chosen bad works. This view does give atheists and agnostics a reason to be moral, as long as they can know which acts are moral or immoral. The problem is that this view conflicts with many Bible verses.

Some passages in the Bible (as well as many Christian churches) seem to endorse predestination:

> What then shall we say? Is God unjust? Not at all! For He says to Moses, "I will have mercy on whom I have mercy, and I will have compassion on whom I have compassion." It does not, therefore, depend on man's desire or effort, but on God's mercy.... God has mercy on whom he wants to have mercy, and he hardens whom he wants to harden. (*Romans* 9:14–18; see also *Ephesians* 1:4–5)

The author of *Romans* (reportedly Paul) realizes that this harsh doctrine might not seem fair, so he quickly adds,

> One of you will say to me: "Then why does God still blame us? For who resists his will?" But who are you, O man, to talk back to God? (*Romans* 9: 19–20)

This retort hardly answers the question. The doctrine of predestination still seems unfair, because people do not have control over whether they end up in Heaven or Hell. It is up to God, who "has mercy on whom he wants to have mercy, and . . . hardens whom he wants to harden."

This dubious doctrine also robs atheists and agnostics (along with everyone else) of any religious reason to be moral. Since God is all-knowing and unchanging, He made up his mind a long time ago about where you would end up, and nothing you do now can change your fate. If you are headed for Hell, no good work can change that. If you are headed for Heaven, no immorality can change that. On this view, then, Heaven and Hell do not really give anyone any reason to be moral, because being moral does not affect where you end up.

Fortunately (?!), the Bible is not consistent. Other passages suggest different views of Heaven and Hell. Unfortunately, these other doctrines also undermine any religious reason for atheists and agnostics to be moral. We already saw *Matthew* 12:31, which says that anyone who blasphemes against the Holy Spirit will never be forgiven. Add that to this lovely sentiment:

> If anyone sins deliberately by rejecting the Savior after knowing the truth of forgiveness, this sin is not covered by Christ's death; there is no way to get rid of it. There will be nothing to look forward to but the terrible punishment of God's awful anger which will consume all his enemies. (*Hebrews* 10:26–27)

I used to be an evangelical Christian. Now I am an atheist. This verse, thus, implies that even Christ's death cannot get me out of Hell. But this gives me nothing to lose by acting immorally and nothing to gain by acting morally. Whether I lie, cheat, and steal—or whether I convert back to Christianity—cannot ever have any effect on my ultimate fate, according to this verse. Hence, Heaven and Hell supply me, among others, with no reason to be moral. It's lucky that I believe in a secular reason to be moral!

Forget about me. What about a confused teenager who wavers back and forth in her Christian beliefs? She is doomed without hope, according to this verse. What about innocent young children? They are also doomed, because of original sin, if they have not accepted their Lord Jesus Christ as their Savior, according to common doctrines based on several Bible verses. That is why children are baptized so early. What about very good atheists, who sacrifice and work hard to help others? Doomed again. They can only be justified (that is, saved) not by works but by faith, at least according to some verses: "a man is justified by faith apart from observing the law" (*Romans* 3:28; see also *Ephesians* 2:8–9). The Christian doctrine is not just that all of these people go to Hell. Christians also hold that God is all-good, so He does not send anyone to Hell who does not deserve it. These two Christian doctrines together imply that all of these people deserve to go to Hell. Forever. That does not sound like morality to me. What about you?

Of course, many Christians deny that they hold this moral view. They have to deny it in order to remain credible. However, it sure seems to follow from common doctrines and the Bible verses that I quoted. If the whole Bible is literally true, then very good atheists all go to Hell and deserve to go there.

Traditional evangelical Christians have a choice. They can follow the Bible and hold that very good atheists all deserve to go to Hell and are headed for Hell eternally. That option is so harsh as to be implausible, if not downright immoral. Or else they can admit that very good atheists do not deserve eternal damnation, but then they need to admit that parts of the Bible are not literally true. You cannot keep your moral bearings without giving up on the literal truth of the whole Bible.

MEANING WHAT?

Fine, you say, so Heaven and Hell are no good as reasons to be moral, but at least they last forever. The problem with avoiding harm to others is that anything I do is finite. If I cheat a rival in order to get a job, he will be harmed unfairly, but how much does that matter? He and I are both going to die anyway. Indeed, our whole species will disappear by evolving into something else. And the Earth is going to be engulfed by the Sun in about four billion years. So a little harm now does not make any real difference to the big picture. It's nothing compared to eternity. And avoiding harm also doesn't matter. It's all meaningless. In contrast, God does make an infinite difference. So do eternal salvation and damnation. That is why only religion gives a truly meaningful reason to be moral, according to some theists.

My response recalls Alvie Singer's mom in Woody Allen's movie, *Annie Hall*. As a young boy in Brooklyn, Alvie is suffering existential angst as a result of discovering that the universe is expanding. Alvie's mom quips, "What does that have to do with Brooklyn? Brooklyn is not expanding."

The conflict is between those people who are satisfied to do what they can in the temporary world that they inhabit and other people who feel that morality and all of life are empty and ultimately meaningless unless they have some kind of eternal significance. These conditions can be called *finiphilia* and *infiniphilia*, respectively. Finiphiles love their finite world but still grant that infinite gains are meaningful. The conflict arises only because infiniphiles (or infiniphiliacs?) love the infinite so much that they deny that finite goods, harms, and lives have any meaning at all in the face of eternity.

The problem with infiniphilia is that it robs us of any incentive to improve this finite world. Indeed, it gives us reason to destroy this finite world if we need to do so in order to reach an eternal Heaven. Just think of suicide bombers. If this is the best that theism can do, then it cannot provide a sound reason to be moral. Nor can it provide meaning in this life.

On the secular view, the reason to be moral lies in avoiding or preventing harm to others. The others who are benefited will eventually die, but that does not show that nothing was accomplished. Those individuals and their lives were better off because someone chose to act morally instead of immorally, so they were harmed less than they otherwise would have been. That harm is avoided forever, even if other harms occur later. This matters to any caring person. It would be sad if that were not enough reason to be moral. It would also be sad if helping others were not enough to give meaning to our lives. Luckily, it is.

a coherent consensus, then you are justified in believing your moral judgment.

A good model of this general method is a hospital ethics committee. The members of these committees vary in their expertise—medicine, surgery, pediatrics, and so on—as well as in their professions in the hospital—doctors, nurses, social workers, lawyers, administrators, clergy, philosophers—and should include community members as well. The committee members also ideally vary in their culture—Hispanic, Asian, black, and so on—at least in cases where culture becomes relevant. This diversity in expertise and culture enables the committee to consider the many facts as well as the various perspectives that bear on each case.

In addition, members should be required to withdraw when they are too emotional or biased about a particular case before them. The committee should work together for a long period so that they can compare a wide range of cases and learn the skills needed for productive deliberation. In practice, a subcommittee that is on call often needs to make a quick decision based on shared experience, and only later can they present the case to the whole committee at a regular meeting for further discussion. Still, if there is time and need, then they discuss each case fully. When such a diverse, knowledgeable, and impartial group reaches consensus about the moral wrongness of a certain act, then they and we are justified in believing that the act is indeed morally wrong.

An example should help to bring these abstractions down to earth. This case illustrates a real problem that hospital ethics committees have faced many times and that has been controversial in the past.

Imagine that a doctor thinks a female patient with breast cancer should get a single mastectomy. The doctor realizes that an alternative treatment would be a lumpectomy plus radiation, but the survival rate of the lumpectomy is only 90 percent to 95 percent, whereas the survival rate of the mastectomy is slightly higher: 95 percent to 98 percent. (These figures are for illustration only.) The doctor fears that the patient might choose to take her chances with the radiation treatment, but he thinks that she should not risk it. For this reason, he wants to recommend a mastectomy without telling her about the lumpectomy alternative. He brings this case to the hospital ethics committee, of which you are a member, and asks whether it would be morally wrong not to tell the patient about the possibility of lumpectomy plus radiation.

How can the committee go about answering his question? They need to gather accurate information about recovery rates and difficulties adjusting to prostheses for patients like this one (and not just for patients in general). Then they need to get to know the patient, including not only her level of competence for medical decision making but also her personality and interests. How much will the loss of a breast affect her self-image, confidence, and happiness? The committee might also consider effects on the patient's spouse and family, since the patient's interests are affected by how they react. The patient's religion is also relevant if any proposed treatments conflict with her religious views, as in the case of Jehovah's witnesses who refuse blood transfusions. Next the committee should consider applicable laws and hospital policies, as well as likely effects of changing those policies in various ways. If doctors are allowed to withhold information about alternative treatments in cases like this one, how would that general policy affect public confidence in doctors? The committee should also listen to the doctor and any other personnel who have moral or other qualms about one or another of the treatments or about withholding information. Not all of this information is needed in every case, but it should be available and considered whenever it is relevant and might affect the decision.

After gathering this information, the committee needs to deliberate long enough and carefully enough to reach consensus. This might or might not take a long time, but it is often crucial. It can be useful for them to think through various principles about when it is morally permissible for a doctor to withhold treatment information. They should try to imagine themselves in the positions of the various people involved, especially the patient and doctor. Would you feel mistreated if a doctor did that to you? They should also consider analogies: What if your investment counselor or stock broker intentionally withheld information about a potential investment because he thought it was too risky for you even though he thought you might want to take that risk? Would that be morally justified? Exercises and analogies like these help to increase impartiality and focus on the morally relevant features.

The committee should try to include a wide variety of moral perspectives. In this case, it seems crucial for the committee to include some women who might have a better sense of why this patient might be willing to increase her risk of death in order to avoid a mastectomy. It should also include doctors and nurses who might appreciate why the doctor wants to withhold information, hospital administrators and lawyers who could provide insight into hospital policies and potential effects of violating or changing them, and also, of course, representatives of various religions—as well as a philosopher with training in moral theory.

If this diverse committee reaches consensus after gathering information and deliberating carefully and thoroughly, then they can be justified in forming and holding that moral judgment. They can even have moral knowledge, if they get it right. There are, of course, no guarantees that they will reach the correct conclusion, but sometimes it seems obvious that they do, because even initial opponents come over to the consensus position after feeling the force of the arguments. This consensus won't always emerge, but often it does. When it does, they can obtain justified moral belief and even moral knowledge.

In our illustrative case, consensus was reached. Although in the past doctors often used to withhold information about alternative treatments that they thought inadvisable, after many hospital ethics committees discussed many such cases, a strong consensus emerged that a competent patient must be told about all alternative treatments that would be medically acceptable and not irrational for the patient to choose. This requirement is now written into law in many jurisdictions. That history shows that this procedure really can work to produce shared answers to previously controversial moral questions.

It is crucial here that such hospital ethics committees have no need to cite the Bible or refer to God in any way. They do not need to pray together or have any religious experience or revelation. Some committee members can even be atheists and agnostics. This shows how justified moral belief and even moral knowledge can be achieved in controversial cases without religious belief.

Furthermore, it usually would not help them to refer to God or to religion. Suppose one committee member cites a religious experience, perhaps while praying. Why should the other members accept that personal revelation? Contemplative prayer can aid reflection in some people, but that reflection will still need to be explained to the rest of the committee. Next, suppose a member cites the Bible. Why do the others have to believe what the Bible says? Even if they all agree that the Bible is the inerrant word of God, they can always reinterpret the Bible or apply it in a different way to the case at hand. Suppose a member says that his minister told him what the Bible really means. Why should anyone agree with that particular minister, who is, after all, a fallible human? Of course, some scripture or religious authority might guide them if they all adhere to the same religious perspective, but that would defeat the purpose of diversity on the committee. Only one moral perspective would be represented, and that perspective might be distorted. On a diverse committee with multiple perspectives, religious documents and ministers should be trusted *only* if their moral proclamations are plausible and supported by independent reasons that everyone can recognize. Often they are, but then it is those independent reasons that help the committee come to know what is morally right or wrong.

Secular moralists conclude that God and religious belief are not needed for moral knowledge. In this way, atheists and agnostics can know what is morally right or wrong just as much as theists do.

THE GOOD BOOK

I would never deny that there are serious limitations and questions for the secular method of forming moral judgments in difficult cases. Life is hard. The question, however, is whether religion really makes life and moral problems any easier. I will argue to the contrary that religion makes it even harder to know what is morally right or wrong.

Consider the divine command theory: How can we know what God commands? Suppose you wonder whether it is immoral to leave home without a cross (say, on a chain around your neck). If the divine command theory is correct, then you need to find out whether God commanded you not to leave home without a cross. You cannot settle this issue simply by finding out that leaving home without a cross causes no harm to anyone, unless you assume that God's only command is not to cause harm, but why would you assume that? You also cannot rely on your moral intuitions unless you have adequate reason to think that your intuitions accurately reflect every divine command. Even if your moral intuition tells you that nothing is immoral about leaving home without a cross, there might be some divine command that you missed which makes it wrong to leave home without a cross. This possibility exists unless your own intuitions capture every divine command, but you cannot know that without already knowing all that God commanded. You also cannot rely on testimony from other people, unless you have some adequate reason to think that they are inspired by God or that their intuitions reflect every divine command; but again you cannot have any such reason without already knowing all that God commanded. Thus, the divine command theory makes it very hard or even impossible to tell whether it is morally wrong to leave home without a cross.

The problem is obviously that we have no sound way to determine what God commanded. Even if theists could show that God exists, that still would not help at all in determining what God commands. God is, after all, supposed to be a profound mystery, whose ways are not our ways. His commands, then, might be very far from what we think He ought to command.

Divine command theorists often announce what God commands, as if they know. The commands that they ascribe to God are often (though not always) plausible. However, what makes us and them accept that God commands those actions rather than others is that we already and independently have a reason to believe that certain acts are immoral. Assuming God is good, of course God would command us not to rape. But the only way we can know that God would issue that command is that we already know that rape is immoral. There is no way to know what God does or would command without already knowing what is morally right and wrong.

Divine command theorists sometimes say that we can know what God commands by knowing God's nature: "God's own holy and loving nature supplies the absolute standard against which all actions are measured."[65] But is it fair to require mere mortals to be like God (as in *Matthew* 5:48)? In any case, it is not clear how we are supposed to know God's infinite and incomprehensible nature well enough to use it as a standard in real life in this world. God is so different from us that what is good for him might not be good for us. Even if it is good for God to be faithful or punitive, for example, it does not follow that it is good for us humans to be faithful or punitive. We are so different from God in so many ways that God's standards of goodness might be very different from our own standards of goodness, as theists themselves often suggest when trying to explain how a good God could allow so much apparently uncompensated suffering in the world.[66] For all of these reasons, we cannot know God's commands by knowing His nature.

Religious people might try to know divine commands directly through prayer or listening to God. That is really dangerous. Remember David Berkowitz. You need some way to tell whether God is speaking instead of Satan or some delusion. It is hard to see how to do that if you lack any independent moral compass in advance.

Finally, we might seem to be able to know divine commands through Holy Scriptures. D'Souza, for example, claims, "In various religions, traditional morality is contained in some form of a written code. The best example is the Ten Commandments."[67] One question, of course, is how D'Souza determines which code is best. However that question is answered, the Ten Commandments hardly contains all of traditional morality. Since most people today do not remember them, here they are from *Exodus* 20:3–17 (compare *Deuteronomy* 5:6–21):

1. You shall have no other gods before me.
2. You shall not make for yourself an idol in the form of anything in heaven above or on the earth beneath or in the waters below. You shall not bow down to them or worship them; for I, the Lord your God, am a jealous God, punishing the children for the sin of the fathers to the third and fourth generation of those who hate me,

but showing love to a thousand generations of those who love me and keep my commandments.

3. You shall not misuse the name of the Lord your God, for the Lord will not hold anyone guiltless who misuses his name.

4. Remember the Sabbath day by keeping it holy. Six days you shall labor and do all your work, but the seventh day is a Sabbath to the Lord your God. On it you shall not do any work, neither you, nor your son or daughter, nor your manservant or maidservant, nor your animals, nor the alien within your gates. For in six days the Lord made the heavens and the earth, the sea, and all that is in them, but he rested on the seventh day. Therefore the Lord blessed the Sabbath day and made it holy.

5. Honor your father and your mother, so that you may live long in the land the Lord your God is giving you.

6. You shall not murder.

7. You shall not commit adultery.

8. You shall not steal.

9. You shall not give false testimony against your neighbor.

10. You shall not covet your neighbor's house. You shall not covet your neighbor's wife, or his manservant or maidservant, his ox or donkey, or anything that belongs to your neighbor.

Notice the bit in Commandment 2 about "punishing the children for the sin of the fathers." If this is what D'Souza calls "traditional morality," what's so great about it? It is not fair to punish me for what my great-great-great-grandfather did. The same goes for the apparent endorsement of slavery in

Commandments 4 and 10, since "manservant" and "maidservant" are just modern euphemisms for male and female slaves.

Notice also what is missing. There is nothing about not cheating, breaking promises, or hitting other people. There is no mention of caring for children or helping the needy. There is also nothing about incest, necrophilia, cannibalism, or patriotism. Moreover, nothing specifies what counts as murder or stealing, much less coveting. Hence, this list cannot be used to settle any difficult moral issues, much less all of them.

Finally, it is not clear whether the first four commandments are supposed to apply to anyone other than Jews. After all, many non-Jews have no way of knowing which day is the Sabbath. But if these rules apply only to Jews, then they have little to do with morality, which is supposed to apply to all people. For these reasons, the Ten Commandments are not such a great guide to morality after all.

What about the rest of the Bible? Maybe we can find out what is moral or immoral by reading that. Unfortunately, the rest of the Bible contains some horrible moral messages. I already quoted *Romans* 1:27 in the New Testament saying that homosexual love is an "indecent...perversion" as well as *Leviticus* 20:13 (see also 18:22) saying that homosexuals "must be put to death." I also quoted *Deuteronomy* 13:6–9 (see also *Exodus* 22:20, *2 Chronicles* 15:13, *Hebrews* 10:28–29) on killing non-believers, and *Joshua* 10:40 and 11:20 on genocide commanded by God. Then we saw *Proverbs* 23:13–14 recommending beating children with rods, and *Ephesians* 5:22–24 (plus *Colossians* 3:18, *1 Peter* 3:1, *1 Corinthians* 11:3) demanding that women submit to their husbands in everything. On punishment, I discussed *Genesis* 6 endorsing worldwide punishment by flood and *Revelation* 21:8 on eternal damnation for liars and cowards (does that punishment fit the crime?). Here's a sample of even more moral wisdom from the Bible:

On slavery:

If a man sells his daughter as a servant [that is, slave], she is not to go free as menservants do. (*Exodus* 21:7—How much for your daughter?)

If a man beats his male or female slave with a rod and the slave dies as a direct result, he must be punished, but he is not to be punished if the slave gets up after a day or two, since the slave is his property. (*Exodus* 21:20–21—At least this gives slave-owners incentive to keep their slaves alive for a few days after beating them!)

Slaves, obey your earthly masters in everything; and do it, not only when their eye is on you and to win their favor, but with sincerity of heart and reverence for the Lord. (*Colossians* 3:22; see also *Ephesians* 6:5–8; *1 Timothy* 6:1–3, *Titus* 2:9–10, *1 Peter* 2:18–19—"Everything"? What about demands for sex?)

On women:

When you go to war against your enemies and the Lord your God delivers them into your hands and you take captives, if you notice among the captives a beautiful woman and are attracted to her, you may take her as your wife. (*Deuteronomy* 21:10–11; see also 20:14—What if I prefer a captive girl who is not beautiful?)

As in all the congregations of the saints, women should remain silent in the churches. They are not allowed to speak, but must be in submission, as the Law says. If they want to inquire about something, they should ask their own husbands at home; for it is disgraceful for a woman to speak in the church. (*1 Corinthians* 14:33–35: see also *1 Timothy* 2:12—Female evangelicals, take heed; but silently!)

On divorce:

Anyone who divorces his wife and marries another woman commits adultery against her. And if she divorces her husband and marries another man, she commits adultery. (*Mark* 10:11–12; compare *Matthew* 5:32—This sure boosts the rate of adultery.)

If a man commits adultery with another man's wife—with the wife of his neighbor—both the adulterer and the adulteress must be put to death. (*Leviticus* 20:10—This would reduce modern population problems.)

On family values:

Anyone who curses his father or mother must be put to death. (*Exodus* 21:17; sce also *Leviticus* 20:9; *Deuteronomy* 21:18–21; *Mark* 7:10; *Matthew* 15:4–7—What about victims of child abuse?)

And everyone who has left houses or brothers or sisters or father or mother or children or fields for my sake will receive a hundred times as much and will inherit eternal life. (*Matthew* 19:29: see also *Mark* 10:29–30; *Luke* 18:29–30—Is this bribery for deserting children?)

If anyone comes to me and does not hate his father and mother, his wife and children, his brothers and sisters—yes, even his own life—he cannot be my disciple. (*Luke* 14:26; see also *Matthew* 10:35—"hate"!)

Okay, so maybe I went a little too far with these quotations. I do not want to offend anyone. If I did, I am sorry. But I do want to show how many passages like these occur in the Bible. Bad moral advice is not just an occasional aberration in the Bible. There's lots of it—lots more than I listed.

When I gave some examples like these in a debate with Dinesh D'Souza, he responded, "I guess the Rabbis have a lot to explain." Yes, but so do Christians. Many of the above quotations come from the New Testament. Besides, the New Testament says that the Old Testament laws still apply (*Matthew* 5:18, *Luke* 16:17). At least it is hypocritical to cite the Ten Commandments or "an eye for an eye," but then turn around and dismiss other parts of the Old Testament as if Christianity has nothing to do with that part (the largest part!) of the Bible.

In another debate, Bruce Little honestly admitted, "My job would be a lot easier if passages like those were not in the Bible." Right! Maybe God is testing believers. Christianity is not supposed to be easy. But that retort does not make it any easier to see why anyone should follow the moral advice in these passages.

"You are taking these passages out of context," say religious believers. Well, look for yourself. I did check the textual and historical context of these passages, and it does not make them look much better. Consider, for example, the endorsement of selling your daughter into slavery in *Exodus* 21:7. Here is what follows:

> If she does not please the master who has selected her for himself, he must let her be redeemed. He has no right to sell her to foreigners, because he has broken faith with her. If he selects her for his son, he must grant her the rights of a daughter. If he marries another woman, he must not deprive the first one of

her food, clothing and marital rights. If he does not provide her with these three things, she is to go free, without any payment of money. (*Exodus* 21:8–11)

These limits make life easier for daughters who are sold into slavery, but they are restrictions on the buyer, not the seller of his own daughter. Anyway, they hardly make such sales morally permissible, as the Bible suggests.

What about the historical context? Weren't the rules in *Exodus* an improvement on the previous practice of selling daughters into slavery without such protections? Maybe, but that does not make them good advice for *today*. The question here is whether the Bible can give us reliable moral advice in the modern world, not whether it shed a little light in very dark times (which it did).

Besides, even if some of these passages can be reinterpreted to make them a little more palatable, not all of them can. The demands that slaves and women obey their masters and husbands are unequivocal. So are the condemnation of homosexuality and the endorsement of eternal damnation for liars, cowards, and atheists.

And why reinterpret any of them? The divine command theory suggests that we might as well take them literally. If God commands women not to speak in church, then it is immoral for them to speak in church. Period. No need to reinterpret. The command is the end of the matter. There is no external morality that could tell us how to reinterpret these demands, according to the divine command theory.

I do not cite these passages in order to show disrespect for Christianity, Judaism, or the Bible. On the contrary, it is disrespectful not to take the Bible seriously. It is, after all, the basis for all of Christianity. If the Bible is supposed to be a major source of moral knowledge, then we need to look carefully at what it actually says.

There are, admittedly, also some very nice passages and messages in the Bible. I love the parable of the Good Samaritan (*Luke* 10:30–35), verses like "Love your neighbor as yourself" (*Matthew* 22:39, *Mark* 12:31, *Luke* 10:27, *James* 2:8), and many other New Testament passages about helping the needy (for example, *Ephesians* 4:28, *James* 2:15–16) and peace (for example, *Matthew* 5:39, *Luke* 6:29). These are the only verses that become topics for sermons in the best churches. The verses that I cited above are rarely mentioned in sermons, since it is easier for believers to ignore them.

The point, then, is not that the Bible is a bad book. Like most books written by humans, the Bible is a mixture of good and bad. As such, it cannot serve as a reliable guide to morality. If we follow all of the Bible literally, then we will be led astray into immorality because of passages like those I cited. On the other hand, if we pick and choose which Bible passages to follow, then we need not be led into immorality, and we might even be led toward morality, but we will need to use our prior moral views to guide our choice among the various passages. Either way, the Bible cannot provide a solid foundation for morality or for knowledge of morality. To the contrary, you need morality as a user's guide to the Bible.

In the end, we all need to work with our moral intuitions after testing them against the facts and the perspectives of other people, as in a hospital ethics committee. That method is neither foolproof nor airtight. But there is no real alternative. Religious thinkers need to depend on it just like anyone else. Hence, it is no objection to atheism or agnosticism that they use it, too.

Chapter Eight

WHERE DO WE GO FROM HERE?

Neither do people light a lamp and put it under a bowl. Instead they put it on its stand, and it gives light to everyone in the house. In the same way, let your light shine before men, that they may see your good deeds and praise your Father in Heaven.

(Matthew 5:15–16)

I have argued against five ways to interpret the thesis that there cannot be morality without God. Chapter Two: Belief in God is not needed in order for an individual to be a morally good person. Chapter Three: Belief in God is not needed in order for a society to avoid depravity and disintegration. Chapters Four and Five: God is not needed in order for certain acts to be objectively morally wrong. Chapter Six: Belief in God is not needed in order for us to have a reason to be moral. Chapter Seven: Belief in God is not needed in order for us to know what is morally wrong.

Of course, theists might propose new ways in which morality is supposed to depend on God or on religion. This project is part of an on-going dialogue. Nobody can declare the final word. Still, I hope that my brief survey covers enough and my arguments are strong enough to create serious doubt that morality depends on God or on religion in any way.

SO WHAT?

The next question is why this matters. In which ways would America look different if it embraced a secular harm-based morality instead of a religion-based morality?

A secular harm-based morality might seem to translate into major changes in government policies and civic life within the United States and elsewhere. A religious view of morality and the consequent fear of atheism seem to lie at the very basis of some stands on abortion and contraception, embryonic stem cell research, educational policies (such as teaching evolution and prayer in public schools), public displays of religion (such as exhibiting the Ten Commandments on courthouse walls and including the words "under God" in the Pledge of Allegiance), the death penalty, and, of course, gay marriage and allowing gays to adopt and serve as foster parents. If fear of atheism and identification of morality with religion are undermined by my arguments, then these arguments should affect debates on all of these issues.

The effects will not be straightforwardly liberal or conservative. I have avoided these political labels so far in this book, because they are confused. Some conservatives want to enforce "traditional" values at the national level with constitutional amendments, but other conservatives argue for states' rights that would be limited by those very constitutional amendments. Libertarians call themselves conservative, although they usually disagree with social conservatives on abortion, homosexuality, and drug policy. And, of course, a self-styled conservative who was enthroned by the conservative branch of the conservative party—namely, George W. Bush—oversaw tremendous expansion of government and of the federal deficit. Bush also initiated an adventure in foreign nation-building in Iraq that overturned traditional values embodied in centuries-old prohibitions on preventive war. All of this used to be contrary to conservative creeds. It is not clear what conservatism amounts to any more.

The same goes for liberalism. Many liberals fight for restrictions on pornography and hate speech even though classic liberals were champions of free speech. Liberals often favor regulations that restrict the liberty of businesses and their owners. Some self-styled liberals want to limit religious practices in public places, such as schools and courthouses, as well as how parents choose to educate their children. In college admissions and elsewhere, some kinds of affirmative action are in effect required, whereas other kinds are forbidden, but either way the choice is limited by liberals. Such liberalism has little to do with liberty in any common sense.

My point is not to pick sides in the fight between conservatives and liberals. That dichotomy is dead, dying, or dormant—or at least it should be, in my opinion. Even where there is a clear liberal side and a clear conservative side, it is simplistic to take one side or the other on all issues. Each side usually has part of the truth, and the real task is to uncover that truth. That's not easy, and one reason is that religion has distorted the debates and deepened the divisions.

Instead of picking sides in a false dichotomy, we need to rethink these political issues in terms of harm—that is, pain, death, disability, and so on. When we consider abortion, embryonic stem cell research, the death penalty, prayer in schools, teaching evolution, gay marriage, gay adoptions, and so on, we should not ask which stand is liberal or conservative. We also should not ask which stand is consistent with our religion or with any religion. To determine what is morally right, we should instead ask who gets harmed, how, and how much. The debates should be about how to avoid and prevent harm, not about how to conform to religious dogmas or how to appease religious extremists.

Where will this harm-based discussion lead? That is not clear, but the changes might not be radical. As I have emphasized, many religious people are good and already want to avoid and prevent harm to others. Many of them, like the Amish teenagers, do not let their religious doctrines override their common sense. They might, then, act much as they did before, even if they gave up the divine command theory and any fear of atheism. But at least they would base their positions on the real foundation of morality, which is avoiding and preventing harm.

Other religious people, in contrast, really do base their stands on religious doctrines and on the divine command theory of morality as well as on a resulting fear of atheism. My arguments cut the foundation out from under such positions, so those positions should crumble. Of course, I doubt that extreme theists will respond, "Oh, wow, I never thought of that. I guess you are right. I need to change my whole life." Still, if they followed the arguments this far, then they should at least have less confidence when they criticize atheism and when they base their political positions on the Bible. That lack of confidence might lead them to think again about morality and religion.

We need to think about this together. Good theists are on the same side as atheists and agnostics. We all want to move beyond the culture wars that create antagonism and stifle progress. The question is how to do this. I do not have any definite answers, but I do want to close by mentioning a few initial steps that might help some.

WHAT'S A THEIST TO DO?

Theists can help by fighting antagonism against atheists and agnostics. When religious leaders broadcast nasty insults against atheists and other non-believers, good theists who care about the truth as well as about avoiding harm to other people should stand up and protest. After all, atheists and agnostics are often not present to defend themselves, and they would be dismissed anyway. So atheists and agnostics cannot do it alone. Theists need to help to solve the problem of mutual distrust.

In particular, whenever someone says, "If God is dead, everything is permitted," theists (as well as nontheists) should ask, "Why do you think that?" There is so little basis for this quip that merely asking the question should undo its detrimental effects, at least along with the arguments in this book.

Religious proselytizers often try to convince people to believe in God not (or not only) by giving positive reasons for God but, instead, by inducing fear of nonbelief and of atheism in particular. Potential believers rightly do not want to give up morality or become immoral, so they accept religion in order to avoid the moral nihilism that is supposed to follow from atheism. This negative basis for religious belief is defective both intellectually and practically. Good theists who want their religion to benefit believers without harming nonbelievers should speak up against this common ploy by proselytizers.

Religious believers also need to fight excesses in the name of religion, especially their own religions. When leaders in their religions claim that God is on their side in an unjust war, in opposing embryonic stem cell research, or in denouncing homosexuals and their supporters, good theists within those religions need to speak up to make it clear that these leaders do not speak for their whole congregations. Silence is a disservice not only to the victims of such excesses but also to the more moderate and defensible religious views within those congregations.

When a religious group goes too far, good people who hold religious beliefs need to be ready to separate themselves from that group—not immediately but eventually. An admirable example is Jimmy Carter, who severed his ties with the Southern Baptist Convention (to which more than 40,000 churches belong) when they advocated a literal interpretation of the Bible, declared their opposition to women as pastors, and called for wives to be submissive to their husbands. If Carter had remained in such a group, then he would have compromised his principles of gender equality, his good name would have lent support to a position that he opposed, and his reputation would have been tarnished. If more religious believers showed this kind of courage and leadership, then religious excesses would become less common. That would help religious believers in addition to nonbelievers.

Consider also Carlton Pearson, a graduate of Oral Roberts University who ran an evangelical mega-church. According to some reports,[68] he worried about whether eternal torment was appropriate punishment for his grandparents, who had committed adultery, and for a close friend in his church and ministry, who announced that he was homosexual. The final straw came when Pearson watched a news story about refugees in Rwanda and thought that they must also be going to Hell if they are Muslims. At that moment, he had a revelation that "After death, everyone is redeemed. Everyone." Pearson calls this universalism the "Gospel of Inclusion." He is reportedly writing a book in which he "will vociferously oppose this religious, arrogant, ignorant, spirit of self-righteousness, bigotry and intolerance, that is rampant among us who call ourselves evangelicals." In response, prominent evangelicals have denounced and ostracized Pearson, and his church has diminished in size, but he says that he is still as happy and confident as ever. The point here is that by giving up traditional doctrines of Hell, Pearson avoids many of the problems for religion that I have raised in this book. He also undermines some of the motivation for fearing atheists. Maybe theists can even marry atheists if atheists are not immoral, as I argued, and also not bound for Hell, as Pearson thinks. It took tremendous courage for Pearson to change his religious views publicly. That kind of courage is what we need in order to end the culture wars that divide modern societies.

WHAT'S AN ATHEIST TO DO?

Of course, atheists also need to fight excesses by other atheists. When Christopher Hitchens says, "Religion poisons everything" in the subtitle of his book,[69] instead of cheering or laughing at his jokes or remaining silent, atheists need to point out that this subtitle is inaccurate and insulting. Corrections like this do not undermine solidarity among atheists, if there is any. They support atheism by showing that atheists are not as crude, unfriendly, and dishonest as many theists claim. Atheists cannot expect theists to recognize and stand up against the excesses of religious belief, unless atheists recognize and stand up against the excesses of atheism.

Civility does not mean that atheists should remain silent. Criticism of religious beliefs is often considered impolite or unconstitutional, but it isn't (since the religion clauses of the First Amendment apply only to government). To treat religion like a senile relative whose bizarre statements should not be questioned seriously is neither fair to religious believers nor illuminating for nonbelievers. Atheists need not speak out against every religious claim. When a friend needs to believe in God in order to be able to face a crisis, it is cruel to announce your atheism and argue that the friend's religious views are bunk. Nonetheless, there remain many occasions when atheists can and should speak out. We should not let politicians, in particular, base government policies on religion without being questioned. We should not let religion distort academic and popular discussions. When such occasions arise, atheists need to speak out. This is the only way to pave the road to real progress.

Atheists and agnostics also need to appreciate the many good aspects of religion. I am not talking only about stained glass windows, cathedral architecture, and gospel songs, although I love all of that. "Amazing Grace" is amazing, even if it is only a song. If atheists cannot see that, their lives will be poorer. Even more important, there's wisdom in many sermons and in the Bible. Sometimes you have to dig it out of a lot of surrounding hatred and mythology, but myths often contain important insights into human concerns. Atheists can learn from sermons and from the Bible without believing in God. This should come as no surprise, because religions and preachers would not get far if they failed to maintain some contact with common sense.

It is also important for atheists and agnostics to admit what they cannot provide. In particular, they cannot provide the confidence of religion. People want a goal and guidance for their lives. Otherwise, choices overwhelm. People also want answers to questions. Otherwise, insecurity undermines. Religion provides guidance and answers that these people need. Atheists and agnostics cannot provide such simple certainty. However, the fact that we cannot figure it all out is no reason to postulate God. It is, instead, a reason to be modest and admit that neither you nor I can solve all mysteries. Atheists and agnostics can reduce the need for simple, certain answers by recognizing that we are all in the same boat—we all know very little for sure about many important issues in our lives. Atheists and agnostics need to help people learn to live with widespread uncertainty.

Certainty is not all that atheists lack. It would also be comforting to believe that we will end up in Heaven, if only because it would make problems in this life seem more tolerable. And, when people hurt us or our friends, it would be satisfying to believe that God will get them back—though not with eternal torture. Religious believers also have positive feelings toward a larger group of people who share their religion, but atheists and agnostics lack that kind and degree of social solidarity.

Atheists and agnostics also often lack connection to tradition that can make you sense that many others have agreed with you in the past and will agree with you in the future. Secular people need to recognize what religious people gain from their religion, so that they can think creatively about how to fulfill those needs and desires without belief in God.

Atheists can also learn from religions about how to help people in need. I myself turned to evangelical Christianity after moving from Memphis north to prep school. I was very lonely because my schoolmates made fun of my heavy southern accent. During those rough times, there was one group that always welcomed me warmly and seemed genuinely glad to see me: the Christian fellowship. These Christians helped me in a time of need, and I am grateful. Atheists and agnostics need to learn to reach out as these Christians did.

Churches and religions also do an effective job at inspiring believers to care for others and help others in need. Atheists and agnostics need to learn how to train their children and friends to be more caring. A useful step could be broadcasting the true message that helping the needy is one of the best ways to make yourself happy and give meaning to your life. Secular communities also need to build institutions, such as Ethical Culture and the American Humanist Association, that provide places for atheists to join together in meaningful ceremonies and constructive joint action. These institutions will demonstrate that atheism is not dangerous and does not undermine true morality.

All of this can be done without believing in God, so there is no reason for atheists to downplay this good side of religion. Atheists and agnostics still need to criticize falsehoods in religion as well as the excesses of religion, especially when they lead to harmful government policies. But then atheists and agnostics can still learn from religion about how to accomplish the goals—such as preventing and avoiding harm—that secular and religious people share.

Finally, atheists and agnostics need to turn their lives into examples for others. This theme is common in religious sermons, but it applies to secular people as well. If atheists and agnostics show that they are good people by doing good works, then it will become harder and harder for any theists to get away with saying that atheism leads to immorality.

This final chapter might seem uncomfortably like a sermon, so let me return to my main theme. Morality has nothing essential to do with religion or with God, so atheists need not be immoral in any way. If we can get everyone to recognize this, we will all be better off.

NOTES

PREFACE

Epigraph: All Bible quotations are from the New International Version, unless otherwise noted.

1. Richard Taylor, *Ethics, Faith, and Reason* (Englewood Cliffs, NJ: Prentice-Hall, 1985), 84.

2. William Lane Craig and Walter Sinnott-Armstrong, *God? A Debate between a Christian and an Atheist* (New York: Oxford University Press, 2004).

TEXT

1. www.gallup.com/poll/26611/Some-Americans-Reluctant-Vote-Mormon-72YearOld-Presidential-Candidates.aspx.

2. "Can You Believe It?" *Dartmouth Alumni Magazine* (May, June 2004), 30–33.

3. Craig and Sinnott-Armstrong, *God? A Debate Between a Christian and an Atheist* (New York: Oxford University Press, 2004), 18.

4. Dinesh D'Souza, *What's So Great about Christianity* (Washington, DC: Regnery, 2007), 267, 269, and 272.

5. *Free Inquiry* 8, no. 4 (1988), 16. I owe this quotation and the next two to Larry Crocker.

6. www.catholiceducation.org/articles/apologetics/ap0023.html.

7. www.lcms.org/ca/www/cyclopedia/02/display.asp?t1=A&t2=t.

8. Christopher Hitchens, *God Is Not Great: How Religion Poisons Everything* (New York: Hachette, 2007).

9. Richard Dawkins, *The God Delusion* (New York: Houghton Mifflin, 2006).

10. Sam Harris, *The End of Faith: Religion, Terror, and the Future of Reason* (New York: Norton, 2004).

11. Dan Dennett, *Breaking the Spell* (New York: Penguin, 2006).

12. Richard Swinburne, "What Difference Does God Make to Morality?" in *Is Goodness without God Good Enough?* edited by Robert Garcia and Nathan King (Lanham, MD: Rowman & Littlefield, 2009), 55–156. See also Mark C. Murphy, "Theism, Atheism, and the Explanation of Moral Value," in *Is Goodness without God Good Enough?* ed. Garcia and King, 118.

13. D'Souza, *What's So Great about Christianity*, 226.

14. D'Souza, *What's So Great about Christianity*, xvii.

15. See also James A. Haught, *2000 Years of Disbelief: Famous People with the Courage to Doubt* (New York: Prometheus, 1996).

16. D'Souza, *What's So Great about Christianity*, 214.

17. Twenty-five Points (1920), Point 24. I owe all of the information about Hitler in this paragraph and the next to Larry Crocker.

18. Hitler Speech, Berlin, 24 October 1933.

19. See generally, Richard C. Carrier, "Hitler's Table Talk: Troubling Finds," *German Studies Review* 26, no. 3 (October 2003), 561–76.

20. Hitchens, *God Is Not Great*; Harris, *The End of Faith*; and Dawkins, *The God Delusion*.

21. Gregory Paul, "Cross-National Correlations of Quantifiable Social Health with Popular Religiosity and Secularism in Prosperous Democracies," *Journal of Religion and Society* 7 (2005), 1–17. See also the Human Development Report 2005, by the United Nations Development Programme (New York: Oxford University Press, 2005), which finds many of the most secular societies to be the healthiest.

22. Gary Jensen, "Religious Cosmologies and Homicide Rates among Nations: A Closer Look," *Journal of Religion and Society* 8 (2006), 1–14.

23. C. J. Baier and B. R. E. Wright, " 'If you love me, keep my commandments': A Meta-Analysis of the Effect of Religion on Crime," *Journal of Research in Crime and Delinquency* 38 (2001), 3–21. I owe this reference, as well as much of the science in the rest of this chapter, to B. Spilka, R. W. Hood, B. Hunsberger, and R. Gorsuch, *The Psychology of Religion: An Empirical Approach*, 3rd ed. (New York: Guilford, 2003). Any reader who seeks more details could not find a more careful scholarly source than this standard textbook.

24. B. A. Chadwick and B. L. Top, "Religiosity and Delinquency among LDS Adolescents," *Journal for the Scientific Study of Religion* 32 (1993), 51–67.

25. W. S. Bainbridge, "The Religious Ecology of Deviance," *American Sociological Review* 54 (1989), 288–95.

26. W. S. Bainbridge, "Crime, Delinquency, and Religion," in *Religion and Mental Health*, edited by J. F. Schumaker (New York: Oxford University Press, 1992), 199–210.

27. See the discussion of Shariff and Norenzayan (2007) in the text accompanying note 52 below.

28. A. W. R. Sipe, *Sex, Priests, and Power: Anatomy of a Crisis* (New York: Brunner/Mazel, 1995).

29. J. T. Chibnall, J. Wolf, and P. N. Duckro, "A National Survey of the Sexual Trauma Experiences of Catholic Nuns," *Review of Religious Research* 40 (1998), 142–67.

30. For a summary of such surveys, see Spilka et al., *The Psychology of Religion*, 439–43.

31. M. B. Brinkerhoff, E. Grandin, and E. Lupri, "Disaffiliation: Some Notes on 'Falling from the Faith,'" *Sociological Analysis* 41 (1992), 15–31.

32. R. Stout-Miller, L. S. Miller, and M. R. Langenbrunner, "Religiosity and Child Sexual Abuse: A Risk Factor Assessment," *Journal of Child Sexual Abuse* 6 (1997), 15–34.

33. For a summary of studies on both sides, see Spilka et al., *The Psychology of Religion*, 420–22.

34. Janet E. Rosenbaum, "Reborn a Virgin: Adolescents' Retracting of Virginity Pledges and Sexual Histories," *American Journal of Public Health* 96, no. 6 (2006), 1096–103.

35. H. Hartshorne and M. A. May, *Studies in the Nature of Character, Volume 1: Studies in Deceit, Volume 2: Studies in Service and Self-Control* (New York: Macmillan, 1928/1929).

36. R. D. Perrin, "Religiosity and Honesty," *Review of Religious Research* 41 (2000), 534–44.

37. D'Souza, *What's So Great about Christianity*, 78. See also 268.

38. D. M. Wulff, *Psychology of Religion: Classic and Contemporary Views*, 2nd ed. (New York: Wiley, 1997), 223.

39. Spilka et al., *The Psychology of Religion*, 459. See also 458–78, which summarize numerous studies; and C. D. Batson, P. A. Schoenrade, and L. W. Ventis, *Religion and the Individual: A Socio-Psychological Perspective* (Oxford: Oxford University Press, 1993).

40. Ian Hansen and Ara Norenzayan, "Yang and Yin and Heaven and Hell: Untangling the Complex Relationship between Religion and Intolerance," in *Where God and Science Meet: How the Brain and Evolutionary Studies Alter Our Understanding of Religion*, edited by P. McNamara (Westport, CT: Praeger, 2006), Vol. 3.

41. Spilka et al., *The Psychology of Religion*, 466 and 472.

42. Arthur C. Brooks, *Who Really Cares* (New York: Basic Books, 2006), 34.

43. Brooks, *Who Really Cares*, 34. This figure is for the year 2000.

44. Brooks, *Who Really Cares*, 38.

45. Brooks, *Who Really Cares*, 42. See also 26–29 and 94.

46. Brooks, *Who Really Cares*, 186.

47. Brooks, *Who Really Cares*, 214.

48. Spilka et al., *The Psychology of Religion*, p. 447. See also Batson et al., *Religion and the Individual*.

49. Brooks, *Who Really Cares*, 34.

50. Brooks, *Who Really Cares*, 20, his italics. See also 6 and 25.

51. Brooks, *Who Really Cares*, 55.

52. Azim F. Shariff and Ara Norenzayan, "God Is Watching You: Priming God Concepts Increases Prosocial Behavior in an Anonymous Economic Game," *Psychological Science* 18, no. 9 (2007), 803–9. See also J. C. Ortberg, R. L. Gorsuch, and G. J. Kim, "Changing Attitude and Moral Obligation: Their Independent Effects on Behavior," *Journal for the Scientific Study of Religion* 40 (2001), 489–96.

53. Thomas Hobbes, *Leviathan*, Part 1, Ch. 13.

54. Bernard Gert, *Common Morality* (New York: Oxford University Press, 2004) and *Morality, Revised Edition* (New York: Oxford University Press, 2005). Much of my argument in this chapter and also in Chapter Six is greatly indebted to Gert.

55. A popular presentation of some of these data can be found in Marc Hauser, *Moral Minds: How Nature Designed Our Universal Sense of Right and Wrong* (New York: Ecco, 2006).

56. See, for example, Jonathan Haidt and Jesse Graham, "When Morality Opposes Justice: Conservatives Have Moral Intuitions that Liberals May Not Recognize," *Social Justice Research* 20 (2007), 98–116.

57. For an example of such a theory, see Swinburne, "What Difference Does God Make to Morality?" in *Is Goodness without God Good Enough?* ed. Garcia and King.

58. D'Souza, *What's So Great about Christianity*, 233. See also C. S. Lewis, *Mere Christianity* (London: G. Bles, 1952).

59. See Louise Anthony, "Atheism as Perfect Piety" in *Is Goodness without God Good Enough?* ed. Garcia and King.

60. Larry Nucci, "Children's Conceptions of Morality, Social Conventions, and Religious Prescriptions" in *Moral Dilemmas: Philosophical and Psychological Reconsiderations of the Development of Moral Reasoning*, edited by C. Harding (Chicago: Precedent Press, 1986).

61. Martin L. Hoffman, *Empathy and Moral Development: Implications for Caring and Justice* (Cambridge: Cambridge University Press, 2001).

62. This account of reasons comes from Bernard Gert, *Common Morality*.

63. William Lane Craig, "Opening Statement" in *Is Goodness without God Good Enough?* ed. Garcia and King.

64. For example, in Walter Sinnott-Armstrong, *Moral Skepticisms* (New York: Oxford University Press, 2006), chap. 10. For those who know this work, I should mention that all of my epistemic claims in the present book should be taken to be relative to the modest contrast class.

65. Craig, "Opening Statement" in *Is Goodness without God Good Enough?* ed. Garcia and King, p. 30. Compare *Matthew* 19:17: "There is only One who is good."

66. See my chapter 4 in Craig and Sinnott-Armstrong, *God?*

67. D'Souza, *What's So Great about Christianity*, 252.

68. See www.newdimensions.us/, http://www.msnbc.msn.com/id/14337492/, and http://earnestlycontending.blogspot.com/2007/06/reverand-carlton-pearson-from-oral.html.

69. Hitchens, *God Is Not Great*.

INDEX

INDEX OF BIBLICAL PASSAGES